WALKING C(

LAKELAN
Patterdale

Paul Hannon

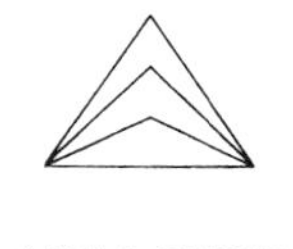

HILLSIDE

WALKING COUNTRY

LAKELAND FELLS

Patterdale & the East

Paul Hannon

HILLSIDE

HILLSIDE
PUBLICATIONS
11 Nessfield Grove
Keighley
West Yorkshire
BD22 6NU

First published 1998

ISBN 1 870141 61 X

Cover illustrations:
Saint Sunday Crag and Helvellyn from Angle Tarn;
Striding Edge, Helvellyn
Back cover: Steel Knotts from Hallin Fell, Martindale
(Paul Hannon/Big Country Picture Library)

Page 1: Saint Sunday Crag from the head of Ullswater
Page 3: The summit of Place Fell

Printed in Great Britain by
Carnmor Print & Design
95-97 London Road
Preston
Lancashire
PR1 4BA

CONTENTS

INTRODUCTION

The fells of the Lake District are the most impressive and most popular in England. The majority of the National Park's 866 square miles is dominated by its hills, from the rocky fastnesses of Scafell Pike, the summit of England, down to some delightful low-level fells. To do justice to this unique landscape, 100 outstanding fellwalks have been devised and shared among a series of four definitive guidebooks. Together these embrace the best fellwalking in the country, and each guide deals with a logically defined area of Lakeland.

The walks within this volume cover the eastern part of the National Park, with Ullswater as the focal point. The most popular bases are Patterdale, Glenridding and Pooley Bridge, and some of the best known fells include Helvellyn, High Street and Fairfield. The three companion guides feature Ambleside & the South; Keswick & the North; and Buttermere & the West.

Although any number of more demanding walks can be planned by enthusiasts, the aim of this series is to provide a varied range of outings within the scope of most walkers. Thus a limit of around 10 miles and 3500 feet of ascent per walk has been set: most walks are in fact well within these bounds. A feature of these walks is their variety, so that ridgewalks alternate with valley approaches, there are steep climbs, gentle climbs, routes that include mountain tarns and waterfalls. All share the character that makes the Lakeland Fells so special.

The great majority of the Lakeland Fells is freely open to walkers, though many of the routes described are in any case on public rights of way. Any access routes onto the hills are always on rights of way or permitted routes. Please be sensitive when passing near farms and dwellings, and if you must take a dog with you, ensure it is on a lead. While we may have every right to be there, the sheer weight of our numbers means it is particularly important to also act responsibly.

Mountain safety is a subject dealt with in several chunky volumes, and here it should be sufficient to say that the most important elements are to be properly equipped, and realistically aware of the three great limitations of time, physical condition and weather. An ability to use map and compass is strongly recommended, as one can be easily disorientated in mist. In winter conditions the fells take on an entirely different character. In such circumstances even the humblest of fells present new dangers: ice, snow, bitterly cold or gale force winds, and

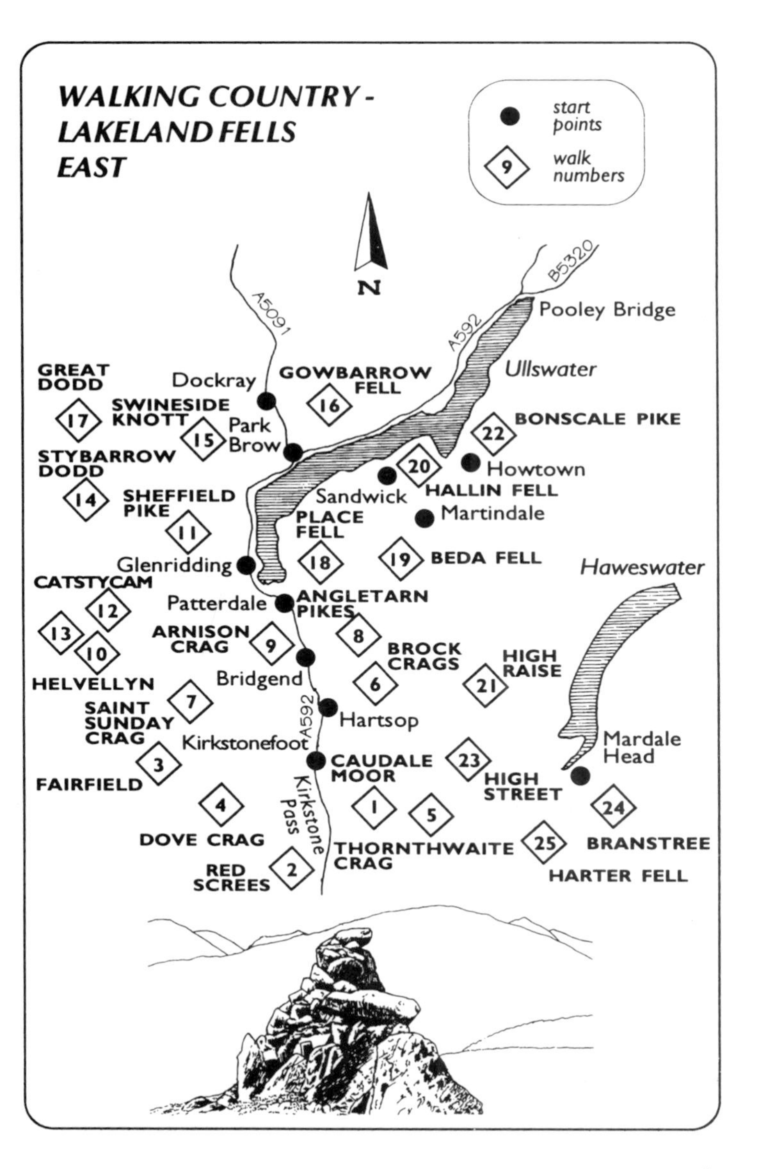
WALKING COUNTRY - LAKELAND FELLS EAST
start points
9
walk numbers
N
A5091
B5320
A592
Pooley Bridge
Ullswater
GREAT DODD
Dockray
GOWBARROW FELL
16
SWINESIDE KNOTT
17
15
Park Brow
BONSCALE PIKE
22
STYBARROW DODD
20
Howtown
Sandwick
HALLIN FELL
14
SHEFFIELD PIKE
PLACE FELL
Martindale
11
Glenridding
18
19
BEDA FELL
Haweswater
CATSTYCAM
Patterdale
ANGLETARN PIKES
12
8
13
ARNISON CRAG
9
BROCK CRAGS
HIGH RAISE
10
HELVELLYN
Bridgend
6
21
SAINT SUNDAY CRAG
7
Hartsop
Mardale Head
Kirkstonefoot
CAUDALE MOOR
23
3
HIGH STREET
FAIRFIELD
Kirkstone Pass
4
1
5
24
DOVE CRAG
THORNTHWAITE CRAG
25
BRANSTREE
RED SCREES
2
HARTER FELL

short daylight hours all demand greater preparation. In true winter conditions one should carry ice axe and crampons and be competent in their use. Don't be put off the winter experience, however, for it is in this season that the fells are seen at their most stunningly beautiful.

The overwhelming popularity of these hills is all too evident to those who set foot upon them. Many paths are worn wide and bare, and in most parts of the district evidence of repair work will be encountered. In recent years this has grown into a major undertaking, with the National Park and the National Trust at the forefront. In most cases the paths are sensitively restored with stone surfaces, a dramatic improvement on the ugly scars they replace. Wherever possible please adhere to the paths old and new, and to any diversions during ongoing pathwork. Additionally, walkers can show respect for our fragile hills by faithfully following zigzags and avoiding insensitive short-cuts; not descending at speed; not walking the fells in enormous groups; and by wearing the lightest footwear that doesn't jeopardise safety.

Most of the walks begin from villages or recognised parking areas, but please be sure not to obstruct local access. Many walks can also be accessed by public transport, so even if you came to the district by car, consider the local bus whenever possible in order not to exacerbate peak season traffic congestion. Stagecoach Cumberland produces an annual timetable which includes numerous seasonal services.

Using the guide

Each walk is self-contained, featuring essential details, sketch map, and route description including comment on features along the way. The basic maps serve merely to identify the location of the routes, for which a 1:25,000 scale map is strongly recommended. Best known for their excellent detail are the Ordnance Survey Outdoor Leisure maps, of which four cover the Lake District:-

4 - English Lakes North West — *5 - English Lakes North East*
6 - English Lakes South West — *7 - English Lakes South East*

(all walks in this guide are on 5, though two briefly overlap onto 7)

Useful for general planning purposes are the Landranger maps at 1:50,000, and just one sheet cover the area:

90 - Penrith, Keswick & Ambleside

The increasingly popular Harvey Maps also cover the district, and their 1:25,000 scale Superwalker maps are available as follows:

North West Lakeland — *Western Lakeland* — *Northern Lakeland*
Eastern Lakeland — *Southern Lakeland* — *Central Lakeland*

SOME USEFUL ADDRESSES

Ramblers' Association 1/5 Wandsworth Road, London SW8 2XX
Tel. 0171-339 8500

Lake District National Park Visitor Centre
Brockhole, Windermere (on A591) Tel. 015394-46601

National Park/Tourist Information
Main Car Park, **Glenridding** Tel. 017684-82414
The Square, **Pooley Bridge** Tel. 017684-86530
Penrith Museum, Middlegate, **Penrith** Tel. 01768-867466

Public Transport
Cumbria Journey Planner - Tel. 01228-606000
National Rail Enquiries - Tel. 0345-484950

Lake District Weather - Tel. 017687-75757

Lake District National Park Authority
Murley Moss, Oxenholme Rd, Kendal LA9 7RL Tel. 01539-724555

Cumbria Tourist Board
Ashleigh, Holly Road, Windermere LA23 2AQ Tel. 015394-44444

Friends of the Lake District
No.3, Yard 77, Highgate, Kendal LA9 4ED Tel. 01539-720788

The National Trust North West Regional Office
The Hollens, Grasmere, Ambleside LA22 9QZ Tel. 015394-35599

The Country Code

• Respect the life and work of the countryside
• Protect wildlife, plants and trees
• Keep to public paths across farmland
• Safeguard water supplies
• Go carefully on country roads
• Keep dogs under control • Guard against all risks of fire
• Fasten all gates • Leave no litter - take it with you
• Make no unnecessary noise
• Leave livestock, crops and machinery alone
• Use gates and stiles to cross fences, hedges and walls

1 CAUDALE MOOR

SUMMITS	
CAUDALE MOOR	*2503ft/763m*
ST. RAVEN'S EDGE	*1945ft/593m*

START *Kirkstonefoot* ***Grid ref.*** *NY 401111*

DISTANCE *6½ miles/10½km* ***ASCENT*** *2020ft/616m*

ORDNANCE SURVEY MAPS
1:50,000 - Landranger 90 *1:25,000 - Outdoor Leisure 5*

ACCESS *Start from a signposted parking area on the A592 half a mile south of the Brotherswater Inn, near the foot of Kirkstone Pass. Alternative starts, on the route, are the National Park car park on the summit of the pass, and the Red Pit car park, part way down the pass. Served by seasonal Bowness-Glenridding buses.*

An inviting spur makes for a highly enjoyable ascent with enchanting views, while the gentle descent has licenced premises half-way down!

S From the start point the two ridges that flank the Kirkstone Pass dominate; Middle Dodd on the west of the pass, and the similarly grassy crest that is to be our route onto Caudale Moor. Begin by walking north along the verge for 250 yards as far as Caudale Bridge, just after the drive to Caudalebeck Farm. Already, Dove Crag has taken on a brilliant stance at the head of Dovedale across the valley. Don't cross the bridge, but take a stile just above the gate on the right, and a good path climbs with the wall above Caudale Beck. At once Brotherswater appears, quickly joined by the pub named after it.

As the wall turns off, the path zigzags up in sunken fashion, soon rising through a collapsed wall and slanting across the fellside. At a fork the main branch swings up to the left to gain the ridge proper. By this stage the head of Ullswater has appeared beyond Brotherswater. The path now scales the ridge in sunken fashion, angling left of its crest and replacing Dovedale views with those into this side valley of Caudale.

This first-class way rises to Caudale Quarry, the old slate quarry it was constructed to serve. This proves to be quite extensive and worthy of a little cautious exploration. The aim now is to regain the ridge, which a fainter path slants back up to achieve. As anticipated, this proves a cracking moment as Dovedale re-appears, with Dove Crag, Hart Crag and Fairfield leading round to Saint Sunday Crag, still, for now, hiding Helvellyn. Red Screes looks increasingly impressive across the cleft of the pass, with the *Kirkstone Pass Inn* visible on the road summit. At once the going seems to ease a little, and an inviting grassy path strikes up the relatively narrow spur of Rough Edge to ease out at a prominent cairn. Two sections of Windermere are now visible, with constantly extending views west to Crinkle Crags, Bowfell and then the Scafells.

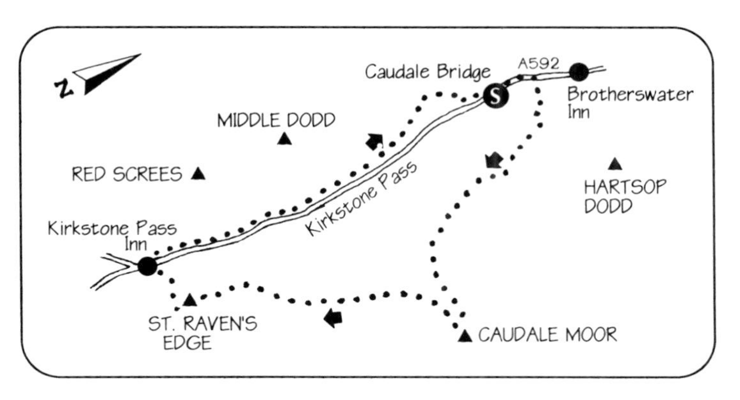

The way runs increasingly faintly around the rim of Caudale Head to a beckoning cairn that has long been in sight. From it a similarly large cairn appears across the gentle slope behind, now very much on Caudale Moor's plateau top. Either take a thin path south-east towards an old wall, and follow a good path (the return route) east; or simply strike east past a cluster of pools. Both options lead to the wall running north-south over the summit. The cairn is found 60 yards beyond it.

Caudale Moor is a mountain of immense girth, and although more prominently named as Stony Cove Pike on modern maps, all travellers across its top will deem 'moor' far more appropriate than 'pike'. The fell despatches ridges which ultimately descend to valley level as far apart as the shores of Brotherswater and Windermere. New sightings on gaining the top are the Ill Bell ridge across the head of Troutbeck valley, and the imposing landmark of Thornthwaite Beacon.

Return by resuming west with the wall from the junction a short 100 yards south-west of the cairn. A good path follows this all the way, enjoying the big mountain line-up ahead, with the individual upthrust of Great Gable unmistakeable. As the way swings down to the left to reveal the pub far below, a thin trod runs 100 yards out to a distinctive cairn. This is the Atkinson Monument, which recalls a former host of the pub - with a second generation later added.

The path then descends uneventfully to a saddle in front of St. Raven's Edge, and most steps have crossed the wall to scale this minor top on its east side. On the crest a brief level walk crosses the marginally highest point to the massive cairn which is the spiritual top, at least. It also explains the glaring gap in the old wall! By this stage Red Screes is now entirely dominant straight across the pass.

Craggy slopes fall away beneath the cairn, so the path runs a little further south to descend a short, stony gully before crossing the wall then descending with it. A brief repaired section is encountered as the path winds down to a stile in the now solid wall, crossing a final enclosure to another stile onto the road by the pub. At 1492ft/455m the Kirkstone Pass is the highest road pass in Lakeland, and the only 'A' class one. Atop it is the *Kirkstone Pass Inn*, one of the highest half-dozen pubs in the land.

The lower section of the descent is more appealing than might be imagined. Suitably refreshed, cross to the car park and a gate at the far end. A modest path continues by the wall, paralleling the road as it begins its dip into the Patterdale valley. At a prominent brow the Kirk Stone itself is passed, a notable landmark particularly when ascending the pass from the north. The path runs on down to the Red Pit car park, then a little further a signposted permissive path joins from the road.

From here the path is a better defined old way, angling splendidly down to gentler slopes. Here it swings away from the beck behind a knoll, briefly a little faintly before approaching a wall descending from Middle Dodd. Use a gap or redundant stile just above, and slant down again. Just short of the bridge in the corner drop right to a ladder-stile, then down to a larger bridge on Kirkstone Beck. Waymarks now send the faint path downstream, before swinging around the pasture to a stile by a gate back onto the road. The start is just a minute to the left.

2 RED SCREES

SUMMITS
MIDDLE DODD 2145ft/654m
RED SCREES 2546ft/776m

START *Kirkstonefoot* ***Grid ref.*** *NY 403118*

DISTANCE *6 miles/9½km* ***ASCENT*** *1935ft/590m*

ORDNANCE SURVEY MAPS
1:50,000 - Landranger 90 *1:25,000 - Outdoor Leisure 5 & 7*

ACCESS *Start from the Brotherswater Inn. Limited roadside parking nearby, and at the adjacent Sykeside campsite (fee). An alternative start is the car park at Cow Bridge a mile further north, and walking the path by Brotherswater to Hartsop Hall (this adds a mile to the total). Served by seasonal Bowness-Glenridding buses.*

Of the trio of pyramidical Dodds rising from Kirkstonefoot, Middle Dodd is the loftiest, and it offers itself as a punishing but very rewarding stairway onto its parent fell Red Screes, one of Lakeland's more extensive heights.

S From the *Brotherswater Inn* turn down the access road into Sykeside campsite, and follow it through the site and across the fields to Hartsop Hall Farm. Turn left in front of the house, and a farm track runs on past some barns, but take a small gate on the left before them. Advance to the barns where a green track heads off through the centre of two fields, crossing Dovedale Beck midway. Alongside a barn at the end, the foot of the open fell is gained beneath High Hartsop Dodd.

Bear left on the wallside path, and through an intervening gate. When the wall drops away to shadow Kirkstone Beck, keep straight on the faint path, bound for the impressive, looming cone of Middle Dodd, in front. Approaching the last cluster of trees, don't advance the final yards to a gate by a sheepfold onto the open fell, but bear left to drop down to a bridge on Caiston Beck, neatly inserted into the wall.

Slant up the pasture to find a good path quickly forming. This rises gently to a descending wall. The path runs on to the Kirkstone Pass road, but at this point leave it to begin the inescapable climb. Assuming the wall remains in a state of collapse, select which side you prefer: it is probably easier to begin on the near side, and cross to the other at an early level break. The pathless haul leads up near a prominent vertical rock outcrop. Angle left to earn a well deserved rest atop it. Looking down the valley, Brotherswater mirrors Place Fell, with Angletarn Pikes part of a splendid array of fells encircling the Hartsop scene. During the climb the retrospective panorama of Brotherswater and its surround of fells is excellent, which is perhaps as well in view of the likely demand for halts.

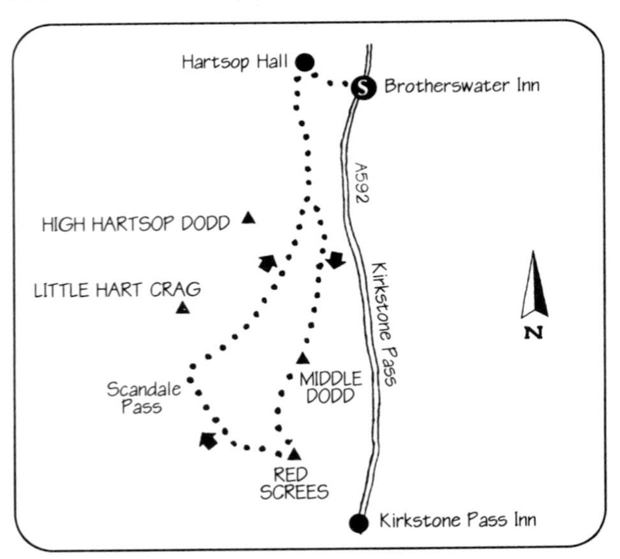

Just above, a wall is crossed at its highest point, and a path comes up from the left. The rocky top of Little Hart Crag is now prominent over to the right, across Caiston Glen, with the Kirkstone road far below. Resume uphill, encountering modestly stony ground but with the gradient less demanding than anticipated. As surrounding higher mountains come into the scene, Saint Sunday Crag is quickly joined by Dove Crag, Hart Crag and Helvellyn. The graceful cone of Ill Bell also appears over the shoulder of Caudale Moor to the left.

The going gradually eases after the opportunity to incorporate basic clambering over rocks, and the dignified summit cairn appears with a level, two minute walk to it, appropriately backed by the great bulk of Red Screes. Approaching the summit, a fine panorama of central peaks slot in over the Scandale Pass, including the Coniston Fells, Harter Fell, Crinkle Crags, Bowfell, and the Scafells with Mickledore well seen.

The path continues along the inviting, outstretched arm reaching down from Red Screes. Briefly level until through an old wall, the path then works gently up around the rim of the impressive north-east combe. During this climb the Scafell massif fully opens out, featuring Great End and the unmistakeable crown of Great Gable; the Langdale Pikes front Bowfell, while Pillar and High Stile join in to the north of Gable.

The summit occupies an airy location atop a dramatic plunge to the Kirkstone road, where model cars appear to make laborious uphill progress. The top is adorned by a large cairn, an Ordnance Survey column, a shelter and a rather more decorative tarn. Red Screes' relative isolation guarantees first-rate views, with ranges and groups to east and west, while distant lake scenery includes the long miles of Windermere to the south.

Leave by heading westwards, the objective being the summit of the Scandale Pass. There is little evidence of a path until lower down, but in clear weather this is no problem. If in doubt, aim due west to cross the low remains of a wall contouring across the fell (visible from the cairn just west of the top). A little further down, a descending wall will be met coming in from the left. This supports a path, which together lead unfailingly down to the crest of the pass, marked by a ladder-stile in the wall.

The second half of the descent begins at once, by turning right on the path which works gently down the upper reaches of Caiston Glen. Soon Caiston Beck is joined, adding a lively sparkle to this easy and very quick return to the valley. A spoil heap by the beck identifies the sight of an old mine level, and across the beck the well defined green rake of the old miners' path can be seen. Our path runs down to join a wall, and eases out to approach a small fold at some gates off the fell proper. Through here the first trees are encountered, and the outward route is rejoined to conclude the walk as it began.

3 FAIRFIELD

SUMMITS
FAIRFIELD 2864ft/873m
HART CRAG 2697ft/822m
HARTSOP ABOVE HOW 1909ft/582m

START *Bridgend* ***Grid ref.*** *NY 399143*

DISTANCE *8 miles/13km* ***ASCENT*** *2625ft/800m*

ORDNANCE SURVEY MAPS
1:50,000 - Landranger 90 *1:25,000 - Outdoor Leisure 5*

ACCESS *Start from Bridgend on the A592 a mile south of Patterdale. Reasonable roadside parking in the vicinity of the phone box at Deepdale Bridge. Served by seasonal Bowness-Glenridding buses.*

Fairfield is best known for the horseshoe walk to which it gives its name, but this excursion, approaching by an enchanting valley and a rocky peak, and returning by a long, gentle ridge, blends outstanding scenery with a far less populated route.

S From the phone box cross the bridge and head along the walled farm road. This rises to a junction in front of a cottage. Take the farm road left through the field. Approaching Deepdale Hall, bear right on the branch behind the farm, thence running along the base of the fell to the rough road's demise at Wall End. A good track continues along the floor of Deepdale, crossing Coldcove Gill by way of slab bridge or ford. Very little height is gained as the sanctuary is penetrated. Ahead, rounded Hart Crag is soon joined by Fairfield, while the ridge of Hartsop above How up to the left is our return skyline walk.

Ultimately the way narrows into a path to penetrate the dalehead, with the exit, Deepdale Hause, appearing at a brow with the knob of Cofa Pike sprouting from Fairfield up above it: Greenhow End on Fairfield towers more directly above us. Still rising only gently above the basin of Mossydale, it runs on through a major complex of glacial moraines.

After breaking through more moraines, a sidestream is crossed and a stony path climbs by a small ravine - the first real uphill work. Suddenly an upland combe is entered, a gem of a hanging valley, with Fairfield's dark crags increasingly frowning above.

The slender green way rises gently to an old, high altitude sheepfold. Here the path makes its final effort, slanting up increasingly steep and scree-draped slopes to effect an exit from the headwall. Contrary to what seems logical, the path doesn't angle back right up gentler grassy slopes to the saddle of the hause, but forges on to steeper, rougher terrain ahead. One or two cairns confirm its increasingly obvious course, culminating in an ungainly clamber onto Deepdale Hause.

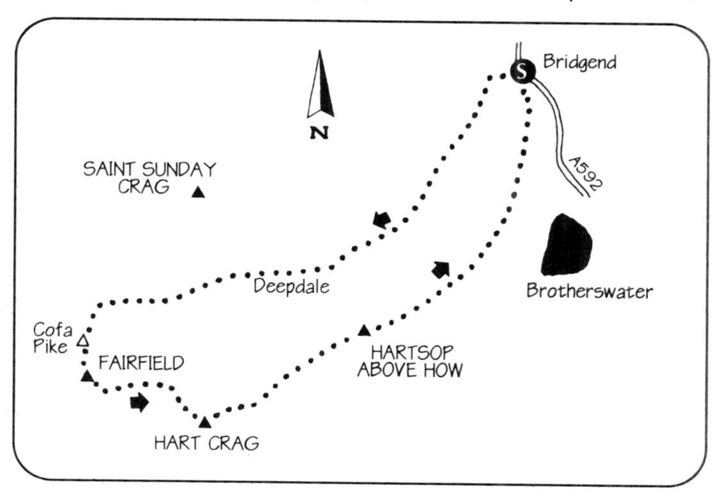

This is a priceless moment as the full might of the Helvellyn massif rears up across the deep gulf of Grisedale, a feast for eyes that have been shackled by the lovely containment of Deepdale. Also appearing for the first time is a vast prospect westwards to the Scafells and Great Gable, while Grisedale Tarn nestles just below. Turn left on the well worn ridge path, immediately engaging Fairfield's steep flanks. This very enjoyable clamber quickly gains the bristly eminence of Cofa Pike, whose crossing demands a steady hold for a few yards if traversing its true crest. Certainly it provides a lively if short-lived interlude before the final stony pull onto Fairfield's broad summit.

Fairfield's extensive top can be confusing in poor conditions, and caution is needed in finding the main summit cairn (a shelter) before the wall of crags lining the head of Deepdale. As a viewpoint Fairfield ranks highly, with an unbroken western skyline beyond miles of lower ground; a striking line-up to the north of the Helvellyn range from a satisfying angle; and an extensive picture eastwards of the High Street group.

An improving, well cairned path heads a good hundred yards south-east from the highest point to round the head of a scree filled gully before striking east en route for Hart Crag. In clear weather only, the path can be vacated in order to appreciate the rugged scenery to the left, where innumerable vantage points overlook the cliffs and gullies around the head of Deepdale. The main path and the explorer's route meet up after turning south to the outcrops above Scrubby Crag, from where only a short drop leads onto the neat defile of Link Hause. It is but a brief climb to Hart Crag, it being necessary to break off the main highway in order to gain one of the identical twin summits up to the right.

Hart Crag is an uncomplicated mountain, exhibiting much that is typical of Lakeland. Rough ground bounds the summit dome with its twin cairns, and all three paths thereto encounter bouldery slopes. Despite its stature Hart Crag is balked by the mass of its big brother across Link Hause, and several other nearby heights of similar altitude take up much of the panorama. To the west however Fairfield's south ridge is successfully overtopped to reveal a striking array of fells centred on the Scafell group.

Leave Hart Crag's north cairn by heading east, crossing over the ridge-path and seeking out a line of cairns guiding a fledgling path downhill. This declines gently before the path asserts itself on steeper ground. Equally assertive is the vertical face of Dove Crag across to the right. The Hartsop above How ridge awaits further below, and the path winds steeply down onto easier ground. This is followed by a second, longer steep section which begins by being ushered down to the right of a craggy knoll.

From the easy ground below, the path gets on with a straightforward walk on a broad, undulating ridge. There are outstanding views all around, with flanks falling roughly to the side valleys of Deepdale and Dovedale. A gentle rise leads to the summit of Hartsop above How, where nature has thoughtfully provided a well-angled backrest; above one's head is the cairn, possibly the smallest and certainly one of the neatest on the fells. This is a perfect vantage point for the triumvirate of Dove Crag, Hart Crag and Fairfield, which present their boldest fronts. Additionally, almost from the very crest Gill Crag begins a vertigo-inducing plunge into Dovedale.

Resuming, the gentle decline of this long curving arm brings increasingly intimate views of the surroundings of Brotherswater and the Patterdale valley, and Ullswater makes a modest appearance. A wall comes in for company but little else changes. Towards the end scattered trees are entered, and at a fence-stile the path delves into deeper woodland. The main path bears left, slanting down through the trees to a ladder-stile out into a field. Cross to join a farm track which leads down to a gate and stile onto the main road exactly at the start.

Greenhow End, Fairfield and Cofa Pike from Deepdale

4 DOVE CRAG

SUMMITS
DOVE CRAG 2598ft/792m
LITTLE HART CRAG 2090ft/637m
HIGH HARTSOP DODD 1701/519m

START *Brotherswater* ***Grid ref.*** *NY 402133*

DISTANCE *7½ miles/12km* ***ASCENT*** *2310ft/704m*

ORDNANCE SURVEY MAPS
1:50,000 - Landranger 90 *1:25,000 - Outdoor Leisure 5*

ACCESS *Start from the large car park on the A591 at Cow Bridge, 2 miles south of Patterdale. An alternative start, saving an easy mile is from Sykeside campsite (parking fee) by the Brotherswater Inn, further south (grid ref. NY 403118). Served by seasonal Bowness-Glenridding buses.*

Dove Crag and Dovedale form an irresistible pairing well seen from the main road by the pub. Adding the return over High Hartsop Dodd, this is a walk not to be missed.

S From the car park a gate admits to a broad track running to Hartsop Hall Farm, along the heavily wooded base of Hartsop above How and initially in the company of the shoreline of Brotherswater. Passing behind the farm, absorb the track from the *Brotherswater Inn* and continue along the wallside to a group of barns.

Remain on this track which runs on to enter Dovedale. To the left is the cone of High Hartsop Dodd, over which the walk will conclude, while ahead is the tantalising prospect of the main objective. Keep faith with the track along the dale floor, dropping down from a knoll to approach the beck at its confluence with Hogget Gill. By this stage Dove Crag has temporarily disappeared. While the track fords Dovedale Beck, keep straight on this bank a further 100 yards to a footbridge.

A good path now heads upstream, climbing gradually to approach the beck beneath some lively falls. Continue up, passing through a gate in a wall and rising to touch the beck again at a welcoming halt, doubly worthwhile as Dove Crag returns dramatically to the scene. Though a thin trod continues along the bank with a line of old fenceposts, here cross the stream and rise to the broad path on the slope just above. Resume left on this, a splendid walk above the stream with the frowning Dove Crag just ahead. The path rises further to arrive beneath a substantial ruin. Here it turns sharp right to climb an increasingly stony gully between converging craggy walls. It becomes a little rougher towards the top before emerging onto easy ground, now level with the crag over to the left.

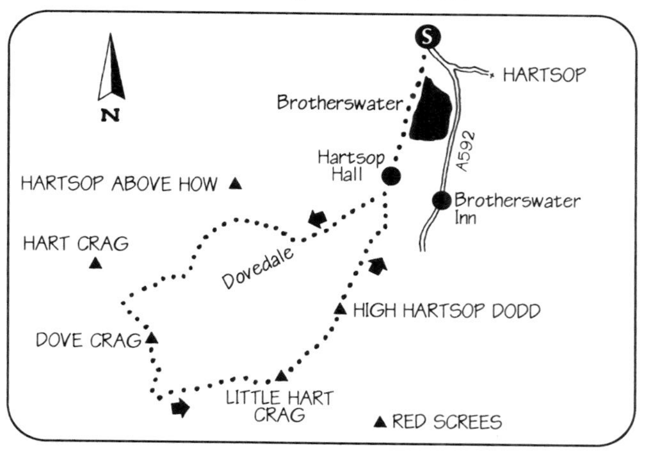

The path rises to tamer surrounds with the rounded top of Hart Crag up above, then passing a small tarn it climbs around the hinterland of Dove Crag into the upland basin of Houndshope Cove. Cairns guide its thinning course up gentle slopes to fade at the col between Dove Crag and Hart Crag. Here the ridge-wall and the Fairfield Horseshoe path are met. Additionally, there is a first view west to the Coniston and Langdale fells. Turn left on the wallside path for a gentle rise to the spacious summit of Dove Crag, which stands a few yards east of the wall. A rocky stance brightens up an otherwise featureless summit, for Dove Crag's rockface now seems in every sense a long way from this broad top. As a viewpoint, Dove Crag's highlight is the well proportioned skyline to the west between Coniston and Buttermere.

Resuming south with the wall, keep on a few minutes past a line of departing fenceposts to where a large, sprawling cairn signals a thinner path striking left. After just 50 or so level yards it reveals a view down into upper Scandale and its pass, with the pillar on High Bakestones just ahead. The path curves left around to this solitary, craftsman-built landmark. The path then descends steeper ground left of it to run along the southern edge of Bakestones Moss. As it swings right to make its way above secretive Scandale Tarn before dropping to Scandale Pass, instead cross directly towards the increasingly shapely profile of Little Hart Crag to locate the path and old fenceposts just in front of the knobbly summit mound.

Here the fence and main path slant down to the right. To gain this fortress-like top, however, keep straight on a thinner path for a two-minute pull up the summit boss to the well-sited cairn on Little Hart Crag. Bulky and lofty neighbours occupy much of the view to east and west, but the fell's position on the north-south watershed permits good views to the valley at Brotherswater one way, and down the length of Scandale's symmetrical bowl to Windermere the other. Appropriately, the sheer face of Dove Crag is also back in the scene.

Leave the cairn by continuing north-east over the adjacent lesser top, then dropping onto a skirting path which sets off down the ridge to High Hartsop Dodd. This delectable stroll runs gently down to take in two cairned tops on this 'non-summit' fell. There is no more than a couple of feet's re-ascent to either, but just beyond the second, the descent proper gets under way. Throughout this stage we are privileged to savour a stunning Dovedale/Dove Crag scene. The path drops down through an old wall and Brotherswater appears in its entirety ahead. The path then quickly encounters the only truly steep section, winding roughly down through outcropping rock before resuming a uniform course.

Interrupted only by a fence-stile, the path slants down the nose of the fell, towards the bottom being deflected by a minor outcrop which would prove a dangerous obstacle if encountered at speed. The final section eases out to drop down to a barn. Pass through its enclosure then off through a couple of fields on a green track, crossing Dovedale Beck and making for the barns at Hartsop Hall. Pass to their right and on the wallside a few yards to a small gate back onto the outward track. From here retrace steps back to the start.

5 THORNTHWAITE CRAG

SUMMITS
HARTSOP DODD 2028ft/618m
CAUDALE MOOR 2503ft/763m
THORNTHWAITE CRAG 2572ft/784m
GRAY CRAG 2293ft/699m

START *Hartsop* ***Grid ref.*** *NY 410130*

DISTANCE *6½ miles/10½km* ***ASCENT*** *2560ft/780m*

ORDNANCE SURVEY MAPS
1:50,000 - Landranger 90 *1:25,000 - Outdoor Leisure 5*

ACCESS *Start from a large parking area at the end of the hamlet of Hartsop, off the A592 Patterdale-Kirkstone road. The main road is served by seasonal Bowness-Glenridding buses.*

Of the several near-identical Dodds rising from the valley floor near Hartsop, Hartsop Dodd's classic mountain cone offers an irresistible challenge as the first of four tops on a superb circuit of the side valley of Pasture Beck.

S From the gate at the rear of the car park turn down to the right to a bridge on Pasture Beck. This sees a track off up Pasture Bottom, but within a minute, after it swings right up to a gate/stile, leave it and instead undertake a wallside climb to a corner stile onto the open fell. Looking back, the hamlet is well seen backed by Brock Crags, with Angletarn Pikes leading the eye towards Ullswater. Over to the east Gray Crag hovers majestically as the final piece of the day's jigsaw.

From the stile a clear path winds up by the wall to gain the ridge-end. This is celebrated by a sudden vista across the Patterdale Valley, with a surprise bird's-eye view of Brotherswater overtopped by the prospect of Dovedale crowned by Dove Crag. As the ascent unfolds the path weaves intelligently about to gain the top, making the climb seem easier than it might have been. It's a gem of a path, with not a cairn in sight until the top is gained.

As the going eases one or two old fenceposts are passed, and the corner of a wall makes a surprise appearance above. Once this is gained the summit cairn is just a minute further. The large cairn is just a few yards from the highest point, where a much smaller pile shelters beneath a wall. Now the high fells dominate, with Caudale Moor inevitably looming large. The path is drawn towards it for a long, high-level ramble in the wall's company.

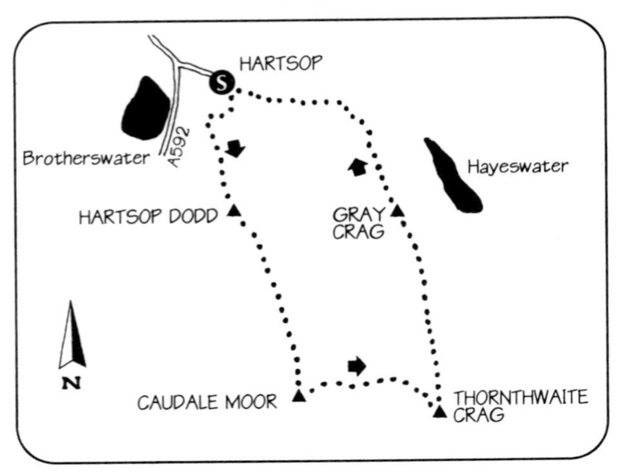

Rising to a wall junction on the plateau-like top, the cairn is found 60 yards east of the wall. Caudale Moor (also known as Stony Cove Pike) is a mountain of immense girth, living up to its name and despatching ridges which descend to valley level as far apart as the shores of Brotherswater and Windermere. Finest new sighting on gaining the top is that of the Ill Bell ridge, across the head of Troutbeck valley.

From the cairn a clear path curves north-east to join the wall heading east, an easy stroll towards the sudden drop to Threshthwaite Mouth, which proves to be a steep but enjoyable clamber. On gaining the pass, a path branches left to offer an escape route into Threshthwaite Cove. Bound for Thornthwaite Crag, however, the slender defile offers little respite from the steepness, for directly opposite the path makes a zigzag clamber up broken ground before slanting away from the old wall. It enjoys a short traverse above steep ground before Thornthwaite Beacon re-appears, now just a couple of minutes away.

A visit here is long remembered thanks to the presence of the famous landmark of its remarkable stone beacon. Though little more than a shoulder of High Street, Thornthwaite Crag is very much at the heart of things, sending envoys to all points of the compass. Leave by following the wall north briefly, before leaving its descent to Threshthwaite Mouth in favour of maintaining the height of this northwards ridge. Long grassy strides are now in order as this splendid walk barely even hints at a gradient.

By the time a collapsed crosswall is reached a clear path has formed. This offers a long, even easier stride on through a second old wall before gaining Gray Crag's lonely summit cairn (the map shows the summit as being on the near side of the wall). Though there has been barely a hint of a gradient in the last mile, when seen from Brock Crags across Hayeswater Gill, Gray Crag assumes an arresting profile. To the west rise the Fairfield and Helvellyn massifs, while much closer, to the right, is the bulky mass of High Street.

Just north of the cairn a clearer path takes over, descending the nose-end above an impressive drop down craggy flanks to Hayeswater, which as the ridge narrows is quickly joined by views left into Pasture Bottom. The path then winds more steeply down the grassy slopes of the ridge-end to a respite above craggy ground. The now slender path slants cleverly down to the right then doubles back beneath the crag, from where the faintest of trods slants down with an old wall to join the broad track from Hayeswater. Turn left down this, which bridges Hayeswater Gill before a steady stroll back round to Hartsop. During this final stage eyes are drawn back to Hartsop Dodd, and up to our horse-shoe based on Threshthwaite Mouth.

Thornthwaite Beacon

6 BROCK CRAGS

SUMMITS	
BROCK CRAGS	*1840ft/561m*

START *Hartsop* ***Grid ref.*** *NY 410130*

DISTANCE *6½ miles/10½km* ***ASCENT*** *1608ft/490m*

ORDNANCE SURVEY MAPS
1:50,000 - Landranger 90 *1:25,000 - Outdoor Leisure 5*

ACCESS *Start from a large parking area at the end of the hamlet of Hartsop, off the A592 Patterdale-Kirkstone road. The main road is served by seasonal Bowness-Glenridding buses.*

Behind the cottages of Hartsop an uncompromising fellside climbs for over a thousand feet before easing out on the summit of Brock Crags. It stands off the beaten track, and this roundabout route appraises the fell and its surrounds before gaining its summit.

S At the end of the car park a track sets off past some sheep pens. To the right is a fine view into Threshthwaite Glen, of which WALK 5 makes a high level circuit. At a fork beyond a cattle-grid turn down the main branch to cross Hayeswater Gill, and the track rises away beneath the flank of Gray Crag. Brock Crags rises steeply across the beck, while looking back there is a first view of Brotherswater, with the Dovedale and Deepdale fells behind. The way rises more gently to close in on the charming waterplay of Hayeswater Gill. Levelling out, the track runs on to the foot of Hayeswater. Long ago appropriated by Penrith for its water supply, this remains a wild place in a bowl of sombre fells.

Cross the bridge on the outflow, and a few yards further the way splits. Take either of the grassy ways rising in front, with the rounded Knott directly above. Soon the line of the original bridle-track is met, slanting up from the left. Bear right on this to enjoy a well-graded slant. Just short of an old wall it swings back left, giving views over Hartsop and Brotherswater to the Fairfield and Helvellyn groups, and also across to the now insignificant looking Brock Crags.

When both the direct paths are encountered cross straight over them and maintain the slant. The head of a side gill is rounded to reach a cairn on the footpath which meets the bridle-track just above. From this high point of the walk look through the saddle beneath Rest Dodd to the northern High Street tops. Turn left on this path which swings down to encounter a peaty interlude then runs on more pleasantly in the company of a wall and fence, contouring round to the colourful crest of Satura Crag. Bannerdale is well seen down to the right.

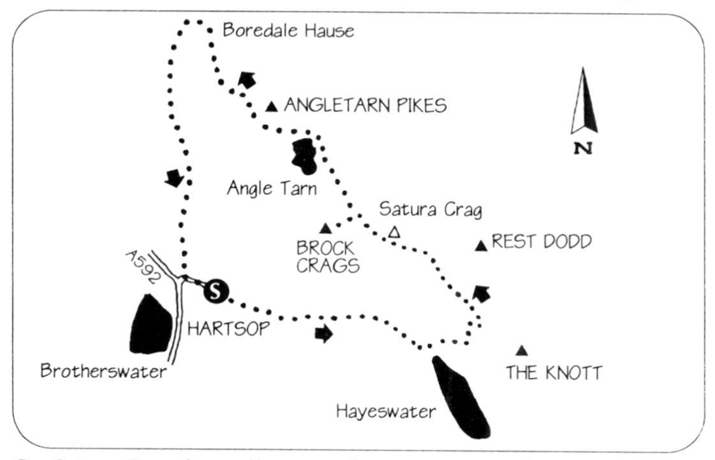

On Satura Crag the wall returns for company until a gate marks the start of the detour onto Brock Crags. Immediately through, a thin path drops left with a crumbling wall. Passing through a staggered wall junction, Angle Tarn appears down to the right, backed by Angletarn Pikes. Keep to the right trod at a fork to join another crumbling wall. On a brow the summit cairn appears ahead, and the thin path crosses the old wall to run between a couple of pools to rise to the sturdy cairn.

This is a stunning moment as numerous sheets of water are revealed: Angle Tarn returns, along with Hayeswater, the head of Ullswater, and a classic bird's-eye view of Brotherswater. Gray Crag appears shapely across the Hayeswater valley, though pride of place goes to the Kirkstonefoot scene behind Brotherswater. To leave, retrace steps to rejoin the Patterdale-High Street path. Turning left, the broad path drops down to run past Angle Tarn, though the path can be avoided a little longer by traversing the grassy ridge immediately above it, atop Buck Crag and its magnificent views down lonely Bannerdale.

Beyond the tarn the path swings round beneath Angletarn Pikes and continues without complication towards Boredale Hause. Though the path divides for a short half-mile, the higher one is only advantageous if tempted to incorporate the twin tops of Angletarn Pikes: certainly there is little reason for denying the pleasure for the modest effort involved (see WALK 8). A feature of special note on the main path is the crossing of the top of Dubhow Beck, with spectacular views down to the valley at Brotherswater.

Beyond a minor trough the path makes its descent to the hause, dropping left to cross the small beck at a sheepfold rather than the true crest of the pass, which is further on. Only a few yards beyond a cairn on its green sward, the path forks: the lesser used left fork is the return route to Hartsop, re-crossing the beck almost immediately. It slants infallibly down the fellside with magnificent views along the length of the Patterdale valley, with the Fairfield group of mountains behind.

At the bottom the obvious continuation is along a broader track, running along the base of the fell in the company of the intake wall. On arrival at a footbridge below the attractive falls of Angletarn Gill, the way becomes a walled lane in a well wooded environment with abundant flora. In time it becomes surfaced before joining the road back into Hartsop just short of the main road.

Angle Tarn, looking to Saint Sunday Crag and Helvellyn

7 SAINT SUNDAY CRAG

SUMMITS	
SAINT SUNDAY CRAG	*2759ft/841m*

START *Patterdale* ***Grid ref.*** *NY 395158*

DISTANCE *7½ miles/12km* ***ASCENT*** *2295ft/700m*

ORDNANCE SURVEY MAPS
1:50,000 - Landranger 90 *1:25,000 - Outdoor Leisure 5*

ACCESS *Start from the village centre. Car park just north of the White Lion. Served by bus from Penrith, with seasonal services from Bowness and Keswick.*

Saint Sunday Crag is held in high esteem by discerning fellwalkers: though part of the Fairfield group, it is sufficiently detached and decidedly elegant to more than justify its own ascent.

S The A592 running south from the village is blest with an adjacent pathway, which is left half a mile beyond the youth hostel, when a path branches off below the cliffs of Arnison Crag to enter Deepdale. Keep straight on past Greenbank Farm to meet the farm road coming in from Deepdale Bridge at Lane Head. Advance on this through the fields to approach Deepdale Hall. Bear right on the branch behind the farm, thence running along the base of the fell to the rough road's demise at Wall End. A good track continues along the floor of Deepdale, crossing Coldcove Gill by way of slab bridge or ford. Very little height is gained as the sanctuary is penetrated. Ahead, rounded Hart Crag is soon joined by Fairfield, while the ridge of Hartsop above How up to the left hems in the southern side of the valley.

Ultimately the way narrows into a path to penetrate the dalehead, with the exit, Deepdale Hause, appearing at a brow with the knob of Cofa Pike sprouting from Fairfield up above it: Greenhow End on Fairfield towers more directly above us. Still rising only gently above the basin of Mossydale, the path runs on through a major complex of glacial moraines. After breaking through more moraines, a sidestream is crossed and a stony path climbs by a small ravine - the first real uphill work. Suddenly an upland combe is entered, a gem of a hanging valley, with Fairfield's dark crags increasingly frowning above.

The slender green way rises gently to an old, high altitude sheepfold. Here the path makes its final effort, slanting up increasingly steep and scree-draped slopes to effect an exit from the headwall. Contrary to what seems logical, the path doesn't angle back right up gentler grassy slopes to the saddle of the hause, but forges on to steeper, rougher terrain ahead. One or two cairns confirm its increasingly obvious course, culminating in an ungainly clamber onto Deepdale Hause.

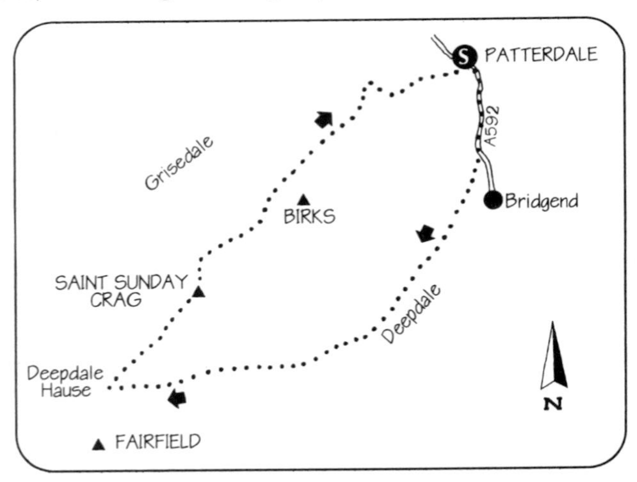

This is a priceless moment as the full might of the Helvellyn massif rears up across the deep gulf of Grisedale, a feast for eyes that have been shackled by the albeit lovely containment of Deepdale. Also appearing for the first time is a vast prospect west to the Scafells and Great Gable, while Grisedale Tarn nestles just below. Back to the right a surprisingly extended but remarkably easy and entirely delightful path runs up the broadening ridge to find the cairn on the summit of Saint Sunday Crag. While the top itself is fairly plain, there are some splendid views to lap up, perhaps inevitably dominated by Helvellyn and Ullswater. The most outstanding, for now, takes in the former, which is ranged impressively with its entourage to the north-west.

The way off Saint Sunday Crag involves tracing the sketchy but cairned path heading slightly east of north towards the edge of the cliffs above Grisedale, where a cairn marks a celebrated viewpoint for Ullswater. Swinging north-east the path becomes infallible, descending through the occasional outcrops of the north-east ridge to a junction on a rather marshy depression. Here the main path bears slightly left, crossing the flank of subsidiary top Birks while losing very little further height: a slim option runs on to the top of Birks.

Ullswater from Saint Sunday Crag

Easy gradients continue high above Grisedale until the path arrives at a wall on Thornhow End. Beyond it the final stage of the descent is a steeply winding path, still with outstanding views over the Ullswater scene. At the bottom it meets a track in the park-like surrounds of Glenamara Park. Turning right, this contours round through scattered trees and across Hag Beck. Beyond a gate a continuing path runs through a bracken pasture to a split alongside Mill Moss, just behind the buildings of Patterdale. Either turn left for the *Patterdale Hotel*, or bear right for the *White Lion*.

8 ANGLETARN PIKES

SUMMITS	
ANGLETARN PIKES	*1860ft/567m*

START *Patterdale* ***Grid ref.*** *NY 395158*

DISTANCE *4½ miles/7km* ***ASCENT*** *1450ft/442m*

ORDNANCE SURVEY MAPS
1:50,000 - Landranger 90 *1:25,000 - Outdoor Leisure 5*

ACCESS *Start from the village centre. Car park just north of the White Lion. Served by bus from Penrith, with seasonal services from Bowness and Keswick.*

Angletarn Pikes is a regular feature of Patterdale valley scenes, made immediately recognisable by its twin summit bumps. This walk's outstanding views are further enhanced by a high level return loop above the less-frequented eastern valleys leading to Martindale.

S Leave Patterdale by the access road branching left over Goldrill Bridge, beyond the *White Lion* at the Kirkstone end of the village. Bearing round to the left, the road ends at a complex of gates, with one on the right granting access to the open fell. The much trodden path slants up to the right, and at an early fork the lower one is appropriate, the higher being used in the return. With implicit ease the path gains height to meet a green track from Hartsop just below a sheepfold. This location could be termed the lower Boredale Hause, for it is the nearest many walkers come to the true pass, which is just up to the left.

The main path crosses the beck just above the fold and heads upwards again, then on through a narrow trough to emerge above the ravine of Dubhow Beck, with magnificent views over Brotherswater to the Kirkstone fells, and across the main valley to the bowl of Deepdale. Here the path effects a distinct fork, and while either will lead to Angle Tarn, it is important to take the upper one when bound for the Pikes. The summit now hovers directly above, just a short climb away.

After rising to enjoy a level stroll, strike up the grassy slope after the low crags. A thin path forms to bear left to gain the rocky summit of the North top of Angletarn Pikes, marked by the tiniest of cairns. This friendly summit was made for gentle scrambling and is further enriched by a fine panorama of the Fairfield and Helvellyn ridges. The slightly lower South top rises across a depression, and should be visited if only for the bird's-eye view of Angle Tarn which the main summit fails to deliver.

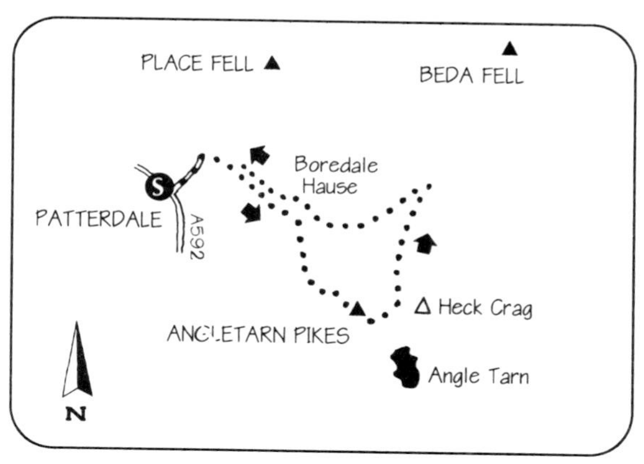

The temptation to wander down to the tarn may be strong, and can easily be incorporated into the walk if desired. The main route, meanwhile, leaves either of the two Pikes by heading east, each top offering a slender trod across the upland plateau. Passing between a cluster of small pools and a prominent grassy alp (560m on the map), bear left behind it to gain a broader path running north-south. An optional bonus here is a detour right, briefly, then out to the well-defined crest of unfrequented Heck Crag.

The main route turns left (north) along the clear path, skirting round the back of Heckcrag Head which also merits a visit for its dramatic headlong view down Bannerdale. Also worth remembering to seek out is the retrospective view of the Pikes' main top, which assumes a remarkable tor-like outline for a short spell. Beyond this point the ridge takes shape for its long journey out to Beda Fell. On this outing however it is vacated a short distance after a very prominent cairn, where the Bannerdale-Boredale Hause bridleway crosses the ridge.

Double sharply back to the left on this excellent path which first traverses the fellside high above the head of Boredale, with the Helvellyn panorama now on parade directly ahead. The path slants cautiously down to approach the crossing of Freeze Beck above a modest ravine, and the castellated summit of Angletarn Pikes makes a dramatic return, a cameo finale. The path then runs quickly down to the wide saddle of Boredale Hause. Instead of trending left to rejoin the outward path, take a thin trod for the summit of the pass where another ruin can be seen.

Although the ruin appears to be an old fold, it is in fact the remains of a chapel. From it a path drops away left for Patterdale, sloping steadily down for 100 yards to a conspicuous cairn at the commencement of the fellside's steep drop. Here the descent proper begins, now on the higher of the two outward paths, from where it can now be appreciated how each is more relevant to its own particular goal.

Magnificent views over the head of Ullswater and into the side valley of Glenridding with its attendant peaks are good reason to put the brakes on this all too rapid return to the valley floor. Leave the fell where it was first gained, and finish the walk as it began.

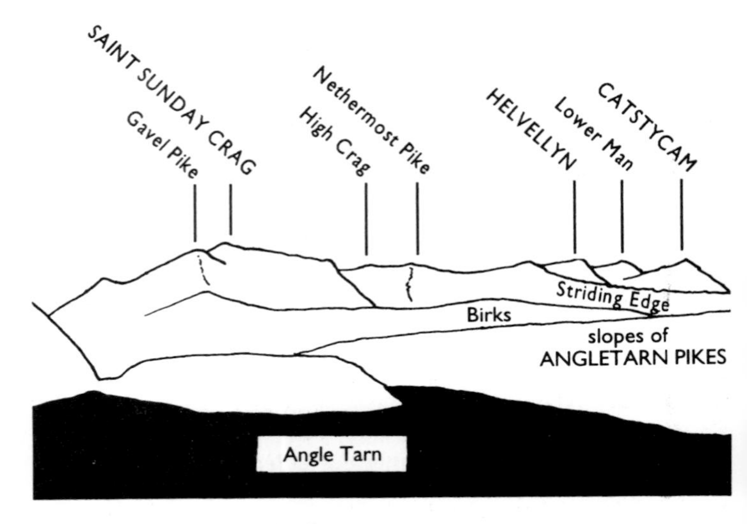

Looking west from Angle Tarn

9 ARNISON CRAG

SUMMITS
ARNISON CRAG 1420ft/433m

START *Patterdale* ***Grid ref.*** *NY 395158*

DISTANCE *4½ miles/7km* ***ASCENT*** *1000ft/305m*

ORDNANCE SURVEY MAPS
1:50,000 - Landranger 90 *1:25,000 - Outdoor Leisure 5*

ACCESS *Start from the village centre. Car park just north of the White Lion. Served by bus from Penrith, with seasonal services from Bowness and Keswick.*

Pint-sized Arnison Crag guards the entrance to Deepdale, and though only the first summit on a seldom trodden three-tiered climb to Saint Sunday Crag, its steep, colourful flanks ensure this is a superb little walk in its own right.

S Leave Patterdale by the public footpath signposted up the rough road by the *White Lion* car park, passing the toilets and curving up to an isolated building. Behind it fork left on a path past Mill Moss. From this level path Arnison Crag rises immediately up to the left. On reaching a wall junction do not go through the gate with the path, but begin the climb by taking a path rising steeply with the wall.

Path and wall remain in tandem for most of the ascent, during which there are glorious retrospective views over Ullswater. A prominent tilted rock is passed, which often sees young groups enjoying abseil training: you may even be tempted into a scramble on this invitingly angled slab. When the wall eventually swings away to the right, shapely Gavel Pike reveals itself ahead, detached from the top of Saint Sunday Crag. Continue uphill, and before reaching the summit the path fades and itself heads off to the right. By this stage however, only a short pull is needed to gain the characterful top. Two rocky tors, each cairned, mark the summit, the main one guarded by a craggy wall.

Arnison Crag excels as a viewpoint for the Patterdale valley, with Ullswater stretching away at one end and Hartsop and its environs sheltering beneath the Kirkstone fells at the other. Westwards the high mountains of the close-at-hand Fairfield group present an imposing scene. This is the direction in which to head, though on a sunny summers' day there will be little desire to hurry away from this welcoming top.

A steep drop resumes the walk, to a depression from where a thin trod heads away towards the next knoll, which is in fact marginally higher than that which has fittingly been conferred the summit. Beyond this top the most slender of trods weaves on along the grassy crest, with the wall still some way down to the right. The ridge ends at a pronounced dog-leg bend at Trough Head, where the flanks of Birks start a climb up to the right, with Saint Sunday Crag directly ahead.

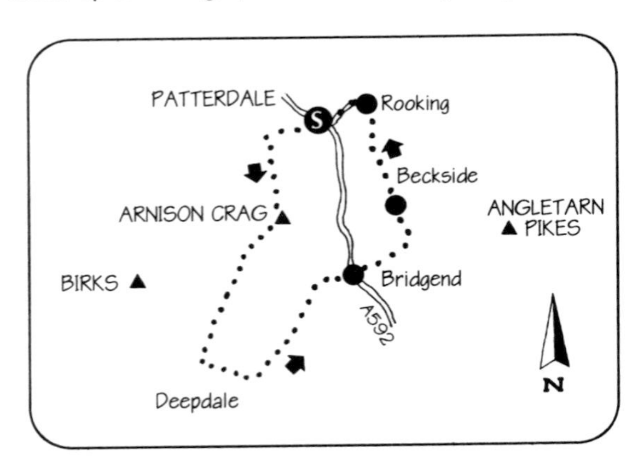

At this point even the trod fades away, and the short descent commences by striking out in the direction of the domes of Dove Crag and Hart Crag across Deepdale. Restrain the decline to a very gradual one while aiming for the part tree-lined Coldcove Gill directly ahead. If reached at the right place it will be crossed with ease, at a break in the trees above a waterfall into a ravine - a completely delightful spot. A path materialises to descend the far bank, running down a grassy tongue before crossing a side beck to join a green path. This works down through bracken in engaging fashion, with the tinkling beck the only company one needs.

All too soon the track up Deepdale is met at a ruinous sheepfold complex. Turning left it soon becomes a rough access road, and shortly merges into the farm drive from Deepdale Hall. After it crosses the field to reach a group of dwellings, turn down its narrow walled course to the right to emerge onto the main road at Bridgend. Cross straight over onto an access road opposite. Past the houses it debouches into a field, and runs increasingly faintly on through two further ones to join another access road. The views from this exposed, flat strath are surprisingly good, and perhaps the finest feature, appropriately, is Arnison Crag itself, presenting a steep craggy wall above the line of buildings at Deepdale. Go left on the farm road, over Goldrill Beck and downstream, well above the beck, to Beckstones.

Pass straight through the yard and out along a broad path, running through scattered trees to approach the attractively located farmstead at Crookabeck. Sheffield Pike forms a fine backdrop to this typical Lakeland scene. A permissive path skirts the buildings to the right, emerging by way of a little footbridge onto the drive. Follow this out to the right, becoming surfaced at Rooking, and enjoying the prospect of the majestic Striding Edge on the skyline high above Patterdale. The side road leads back over Goldrill Beck and into the village.

Looking to Angletarn Pikes from the foot of Coldcove Gill

10 HELVELLYN (A)

SUMMITS
DOLLYWAGGON PIKE 2815ft/858m
NETHERMOST PIKE 2923ft/891m
HELVELLYN 3117ft/950m
STRIDING EDGE 2831ft/863m

START *Patterdale* ***Grid ref.*** *NY 395158*

DISTANCE *10 miles/16km* ***ASCENT*** *3000ft/915m*

ORDNANCE SURVEY MAPS
1:50,000 - Landranger 90 *1:25,000 - Outdoor Leisure 5*

ACCESS *Start from the village centre. Car park just north of the White Lion. Served by bus from Penrith, with seasonal services from Bowness and Keswick.*

The delights of Helvellyn, highest mountain in the country outside of the Scafells, and Striding Edge, the most famous ridge on English mountains, are gained by an unfrequented yet entertaining climb in the heart of some wild country.

S Leave Patterdale by a public footpath past the toilets, opposite the phone box. A track rises away to a building, behind which turn left off it along a thinner path. This runs past Mill Moss, through bracken to a kissing-gate. It then rises away, running on to another such gate. Saint Sunday Crag's underling Birks hovers directly above, while to the right are Birkhouse Moor and Sheffield Pike. Continue on, initially with a wall on the right, then the path runs through the open country of Glenamara Park. Stepping stones lead over Hag Beck and the path swings to the right, contouring on. The views throughout this section are dominated by the sheer loveliness of the upper reach of Ullswater.

At a stile in the adjacent fence, drop down the field to a gate onto the cul-de-sac road into Grisedale. Turning left, this quickly runs on to a junction at a bend. Arrayed impressively ahead are the craggy faces of the fells of this walk, with the neat peak of Dollywaggon Pike succeeded on the right by rounded High Crag, flat-topped Nethermost Pike, and Striding Edge hemming in the valley. Pass through the gate and along the road: when it swings right to Braesteads, keep straight on the rough road which leads in the company of the beck to the last farm, Elmhow. Passing along the front a track runs to a barn, above which a gate gains the base of the open fell.

The broad path runs pleasantly on, eventually crossing the beck at a footbridge just above a confluence and rising to meet another path alongside Ruthwaite Beck. Together they rise steeply to Ruthwaite Lodge, a mid-19th century shooting lodge now serving as a climbers' hut. Its elevated position looking down the length of Grisedale makes this a good place for a break.

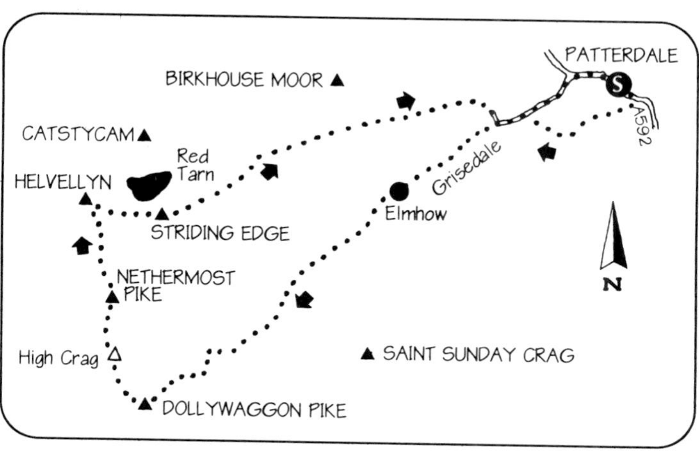

At Ruthwaite Lodge discard the beaten track in favour of a slender green path climbing through bracken, well to the left of the spritely Ruthwaite Beck and a nearer, parallel stream. At once it passes a cave (an old mine level) on the right. When the steepness recedes the slight path slants right towards the sidestream: as the amphitheatre of Ruthwaite Cove is not the objective, the stream need not be crossed. Two means of gaining Dollywaggon Pike's east ridge, known as the Tongue, now present themselves. The first involves contouring left to the crest of Spout Crag, prominent during the climb, the second is to rise with the beck to then slope across to a conspicuous grass gully farther up, the final pull being steep but undemanding.

Despite its intimidating look from the valley, the whole of this route up the Tongue can be accomplished almost with hands in pockets. Knobbly outcrops take over as an increasingly stylish ascent unfolds. Down to the right, little Hard Tarn can be located on a shelf in Ruthwaite Cove, while Catstycam's graceful peak appears over Striding Edge as it climbs to Helvellyn's crest. As the ridge narrows a thin path, superfluous in this upper stage, materialises to cross a grassy arete and so claim the summit of the mountain: on this approach there is little chance of missing the scrappy cairn! A larger cairn stands 30 yards beyond the highest one.

Though big sweeping views to the west might initially capture the eye, the scene is stolen by the eastern escarpment leading northwards over High Crag and Nethermost Pike to Helvellyn itself, with the pyramid of Catstycam showing above the crest of Striding Edge. Such architecture could never have been the work of man!

Helvellyn now beckons, so commence this high level march by heading north over a cairned minor top, with broad grassy slopes on the left and the dramatic eastern plunge on your right. In poor conditions it is wiser to strike west over the gentle dome to drop onto the bridleway. In the first saddle the broad course of the bridleway is actually met, but on climbing again, a lesser path branches right up a stony slope to ease out and fade on the crest of High Crag. Just before its large cairn (just yards from a steep easterly drop), flat-topped Nethermost Pike re-appears with Helvellyn behind. It is a near-level walk onto Nethermost Pike, its cairn being found towards the far end.

In Grisedale, looking to Saint Sunday Crag

Lurking just beyond the cairn is the dramatic plunge of the eastern escarpment, enabling the view to quickly redeem this uninspiring top. Quite outstanding is the prospect of the serrated ridge of Striding Edge across the yawning chasm of Nethermost Cove. At the final dip of Swallow Scarth the bridleway is again encountered, for a short, gentle rise onto Helvellyn itself. A tiny memorial to an aeroplane that landed here in 1926 stands by the last cairn just short of the shelter. A scrappy cairn perched on the edge just yards above the shelter marks the true summit of the fell, narrowly usurping the Ordnance Survey column a little further north.

Helvellyn is the kingpin of Lakeland's loftiest mountain wall, a mighty ridge running north to south and effectively splitting the district in two. Though its two famous edges draw most attention, a contributory factor to Helvellyn's popularity is its reputation as a viewpoint. While not unexpected in view of its altitude, its big advantage is that the immense void of central Lakeland ensures a lengthy gap in high fell country. As a result the various mountain groups of the district are beheld from a well proportioned distance. To the east, Striding Edge and Swirral Edge break boldly away from the mountain, their curving arms sheltering Red Tarn, which faithfully reflects the sombre face of Helvellyn immediately below the summit.

Ruthwaite Lodge

The return by way of Striding Edge is a truly classic route, but in poor conditions (most notably icy underfoot, or high winds) it may be safer to seek an alternative descent. The easiest is to retrace steps on the broad bridleway back over Dollywaggon Pike and down to Grisedale Tarn. Another option is to head north over White Side and descend by the Keppelcove zigzags to Glenridding (see WALK 13).

For the Striding Edge path, double back above the eastern face to the Gough Memorial of 1890. This sturdy monument pays tribute to the remarkable faithfulness of a dog that remained with its owner's body for three months, causing both Wordsworth and Scott to pen moving lines. The roughest part of the walk now ensues as a path makes an ungainly clamber down stony, eroded slopes before gaining the edge.

A slabby finale with good holds leads down onto the saddle, a neat defile where Striding Edge proper begins. At once the only true scramble of the ridge presents itself, a short climb up a chimney with a wealth of good holds. Those unnerved by this have formed a broad escape path around to the right. Atop this clamber, one can quickly opt to cling rigidly to the spiked crest, or take to the parallel path running a few feet below on the north side. The re-ascent from the saddle to its highest point on High Spying How makes Striding Edge a minor top in its own right, though relatively few walkers attain this high point. Also missed by many, though affixed firmly to the crest, is the small Dixon Memorial. This was erected in 1858 in memory of a follower of the Patterdale Foxhounds who fell to his doom.

As the edge decreases in grandeur, most walkers gradually resort to the lower path. In time the jagged edge eases and gently declining ground leads the path to the celebrated 'Hole in the Wall', these days plugged by a stile. On crossing it the Patterdale path at once begins its descent into Grisedale, a long, steady decline with glorious views, both over the valley to Saint Sunday Crag, and across the Patterdale valley to the High Street massif. At the bottom a path junction is reached. Take the right-hand gate off the fell and a steep path descends to a gate onto a farm road. Continue down this to cross Grisedale Beck and up to rejoin the outward route at the bend above. For a more direct finish remain on the narrow road back down into the village.

Patterdale

11 SHEFFIELD PIKE

SUMMITS
GLENRIDDING DODD 1450ft/442m
SHEFFIELD PIKE 2215ft/675m

START *Glenridding* ***Grid ref.*** *NY 386169*

DISTANCE *5 miles/8km* ***ASCENT*** *1875ft/572m*

ORDNANCE SURVEY MAPS
1:50,000 - Landranger 90 *1:25,000 - Outdoor Leisure 5*

ACCESS *Start from the village centre. Large car park. Served by Patterdale-Penrith buses, and seasonal services from Bowness and Keswick.*

Hovering impressively immediately to the north of Glenridding, Sheffield Pike receives far less attention than it deserves, for it offers a fine ascent with glorious views.

S Leave the village centre by Greenside Road, alongside the car park. Rising past the *Travellers Rest* it winds up to the last buildings, several terraces of one-time miners' cottages. After the first pair, a cattle-grid is crossed. Here leave the rough road and rise right on a broad green way towards the higher level terrace. Before the houses, however, take an initially faint path slanting up to the right. This quickly improves and rises into a stony area, and climbing steeply past Blae Crag it improves to gain a knoll atop it.

Here the path swings left for a gentle slant to the neat saddle between Sheffield Pike and its underling Glenridding Dodd. Before getting to grips with the main ascent, it is first worth enjoying the brief detour onto the Dodd. Take the path to the right, rising with the wall past a small scree slope, then running gently on to the large summit cairn. Few fells occupy less space than Glenridding Dodd, but what it lacks on the map it compensates for when beneath one's feet. This charming summit is festooned with heather and rock outcrops, and while here, all should be drawn to several lesser cairns to the east; one in particular indicates an outstanding bird's-eye view of Glenridding beside the head of Ullswater, the whole backed by a fine array of mountains.

Back at the saddle, with a sturdy wall hiding part of the valley of Glencoyne to the north, turn left on an initially faint path up to a crumbled wall. The path quickly takes shape and winds a delectable course up the well defined south-east ridge of the Pike, a spiral stairway through minor outcrops and heather, a particular delight in late summer. Ullswater quickly takes a starring role behind, while there are increasingly super views across to the Helvellyn massif proudly fronted by the peak of Catstycam.

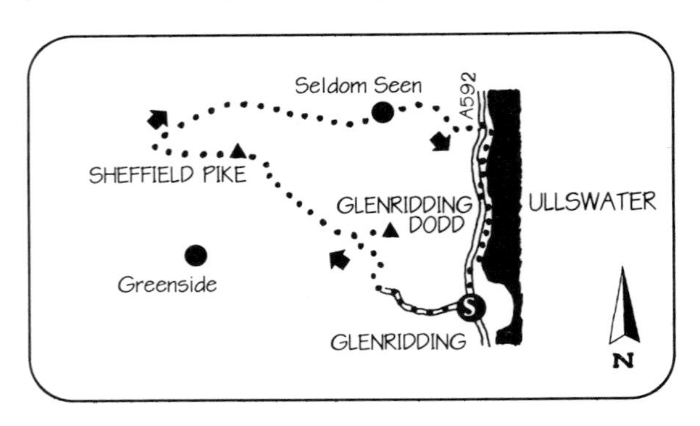

All too soon the going eases at a cairn on Heron Pike, and the path runs on before a shorter pull onto the summit plateau. This surprisingly extensive and in parts peaty top is all that robs the climb of maximum points. The cairn appears some distance away, and the path meanders towards it, at times faintly, to pass a smaller cairn just short of the main one. A stone built shelter sits just to the south of the summit knoll. The vastness of the top deprives any intimate views of the upper Ullswater scene, although it retains a sizeable portion of the lake's lower reaches.

Resume on the path running west, declining only gently to the pronounced saddle at Nick Head. At this path crossroads turn sharp right on a clear path which effects a short but impressive traverse around the steep flank of the fell. In front is the deep bowl of

Glencoyne, while ahead is Ullswater which in its cradle of colourful lower fells is to completely dominate the descent. The path quickly begins a sustained slant down the fellside, a splendid descent on what was originally a quarryman's path from Glencoyne to the workings west of Nick Head.

Ultimately the path reaches a gate in a wall, and resumes with a wall for company to a corner in front of Glencoyne Wood. From the stile into the trees the path drops down to the rear of the secluded terrace at aptly named Seldom Seen. Their access track leads pleasantly out through trees onto the A592 on the shore of Ullswater. Cross to a permissive path and turn right, initially paralleling the road rather than the lakeshore. After briefly being forced onto the road at the sheer cliff face of Stybarrow Crag, the path then leads increasingly attractively back alongside the lake. A final viewpoint is reached before rejoining the road at the edge of the village.

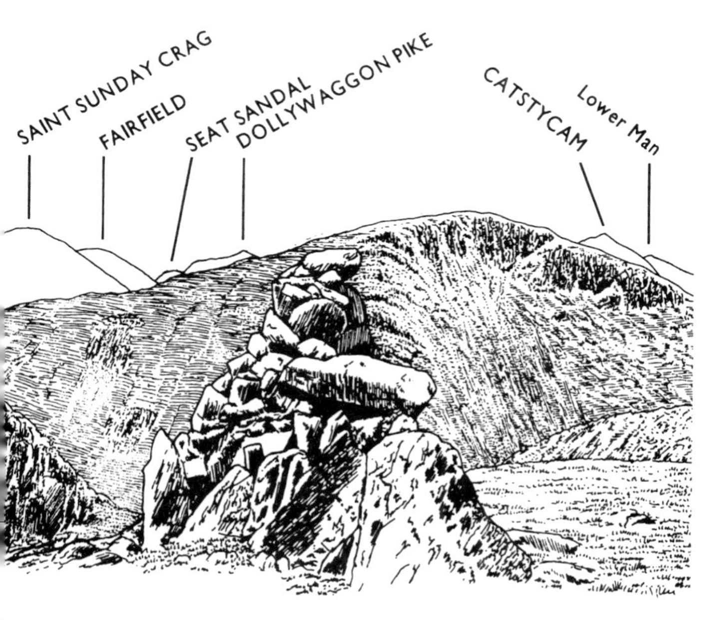

Birkhouse Moor from Glenridding Dodd

12 CATSTYCAM

SUMMITS
CATSTYCAM 2920ft/890m
BIRKHOUSE MOOR 2356ft/718m

START *Glenridding* ***Grid ref.*** *NY 386169*

DISTANCE *7½ miles/12km* ***ASCENT*** *2480ft/756m*

ORDNANCE SURVEY MAPS
1:50,000 - Landranger 90 *1:25,000 - Outdoor Leisure 5*

ACCESS *Start from the village centre. Large car park. Served by Patterdale-Penrith buses, and seasonal services from Bowness and Keswick.*

If Helvellyn is the king of its own group, then Catstycam is its queen, a slender peak with that rare gift of good looks from every direction. Though usually tagged onto a descent from Helvellyn, an individual ascent proves far more rewarding.

S Glenridding is left by the side road alongside the beck from the shops. This develops into a rough road and then becomes a path by the beck, passing a campsite to reach Rattlebeck Bridge. Turn left up the access road rising to Miresbeck, but quickly forking right over a side beck on the track climbing above the house. At a fork keep straight on up, and in front of a small wood turn right on a stony path climbing to a gate/stile onto the open fell.

Shunning the path climbing by the beck, a right turn sees the start of a long, near-level mile under Birkhouse Moor, with Glenridding Beck down to the right and Sheffield Pike across it, rising impressively out of the devastation of the old Greenside lead mines. Rounding a corner the path rises a little to join a higher level path on the course of a former water leat, now directly opposite the upper buildings at Greenside. The environs of the mine workings are quickly left behind, and the lively beck is rejoined at a small footbridge above a small dam.

Cross the bridge and turn downstream on the track, very briefly, and at the first chance clamber stonily left to join a broad, still stony track. Rise left up this, quickly reaching a waymarked fork. While a greener path climbs to the right, opt instead to go left, on the main track which runs improvingly above Red Tarn Beck. This enjoys a super course beneath scrubby, juniper-clad flanks. Rising only gently, proceedings are entirely and appropriately dominated by the fine peak of our goal: nothing else but Catstycam matters now!

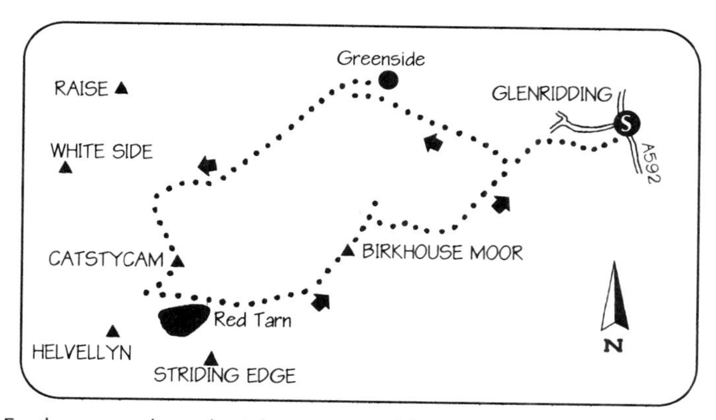

Further on a branch right sees an old pony track take off for the Helvellyn ridge, but forge straight on, rising to approach the concrete dam at Keppel Cove. Ahead are Lower Man and White Side, while our imminent ascent route is seen in profile. Though a direct way crosses the breached dam, you are warned this is entirely at your own risk! Otherwise remain on the track to the sheepfold just above. A thin path takes over, dropping to a breached upper embankment and then rising to some ruins. An old water cut then runs on to the beck. Cross and climb the grassy slope to the base of Catstycam's north-west ridge. Down to the right is the amphitheatre of Brown Cove, which features a tiny tarn above the remains of another, smaller dam.

Despite its appearance from certain vantage points, the ridge is ill defined at the outset, but slant left to join a clear path. This winds unerringly up, and the going improves as the contours taper towards the top. The last section is a firmer path on easier ground, and with a sense of disbelief one finds the summit beneath one's feet: the sensation of having really scaled a mountain is very real.

The reward for gaining this airy summit is a sudden and spectacular picture of the glistening waters of Red Tarn, backed by Striding Edge and the east face of Helvellyn, a masterpiece of nature. Here one can relax, usually in solitude, and observe the gyrations of pedestrians on Striding Edge. At less than a hundred feet below the magic 3000 mark, this delectable cone is the highest mountain entirely within the confines of the old county of Westmorland.

From Catstycam's airy perch a rapidly accomplished descent is made to the saddle preceding the dramatic course of Swirral Edge assaulting the rugged east face of Helvellyn. If opting to change plans and go for Helvellyn (very quickly attained from here), transfer to WALK 13 at this point. Otherwise, take the broad path doubling back down to the left towards the outflow of the tarn. Just short of the outflow ignore the branch left (a direct return to Glenridding) and bear right to cross the stream. Just across stony ground a restored path runs a level course to the ridge beneath the foot of Striding Edge.

A crossroads of paths is reached here, at the celebrated 'Hole in the Wall', which is filled by a stile. Without crossing, go left on the ridge path in the company of the wall, heading for Birkhouse Moor, the natural continuation of Striding Edge. The highest point of Birkhouse Moor is encountered almost without notice, as a scrappy cairn is passed before the wall turns away. At the wall-end remain on the restored path which quickly turns to commence the descent. A lighter

Catstycam from Swirral Edge

path offers a possible diversion by continuing out to Birkhouse Moor's prominent north-east cairn, a satisfying objective. As a vantage point for studying the east face of Helvellyn, Birkhouse Moor excels, and if this cairn is included, then Ullswater is also seen to great advantage.

Return to the main path which now begins its descent, swinging down and round to meet the wall again. A little further down it winds away from the wall and at a circular fold it descends steeply, now almost entirely stepped as it spirals down in the company of tiny Mires Beck. Glenridding is outspread below, backed by the glorious scenery of Ullswater. Ultimately the path crosses the beck above a wall corner and then down to rejoin the outward route at the gate off the fell. Conclude the walk as it began.

Catstycam from Red Tarn Beck

13 HELVELLYN (B)

SUMMITS	
HELVELLYN	*3117ft/950m*
WHITE SIDE	*2831ft/863m*

START *Glenridding* ***Grid ref.*** *NY 386169*

DISTANCE *9 miles/14½km* ***ASCENT*** *2885ft/880m*

ORDNANCE SURVEY MAPS
1:50,000 - Landranger 90 *1:25,000 - Outdoor Leisure 5*

ACCESS *Start from the village centre. Large car park. Served by Patterdale-Penrith buses, and seasonal services from Bowness and Keswick.*

Mighty Helvellyn is a perennial favourite, and this approach by way of Red Tarn Beck culminates in Swirral Edge, an exhilarating yet easy scramble which emerges directly onto its lofty summit plateau.

S Leave Glenridding by the side road alongside the beck from the shops. This develops into a rough road and then becomes a path by the beck, passing a campsite to reach Rattlebeck Bridge. Turn left up the access road rising to Miresbeck, quickly forking right over a side beck on the track climbing above the house. At a fork keep straight on up, and in front of a small wood turn right on a stony path climbing to a gate/stile onto the open fell.

Shunning the path climbing by the beck, a right turn sees the start of a long, near-level mile under Birkhouse Moor, with Glenridding Beck down to the right and Sheffield Pike across it, rising impressively out of the devastation of the old Greenside lead mines. Rounding a corner the path rises a little to join a higher level path on the course of a former water leat, now directly opposite the upper buildings at Greenside. The environs of the mine workings are quickly left behind, and the lively beck is rejoined at a small footbridge above a small dam.

Don't cross the bridge but remain on the south side of the beck. Disinclined to gain any discernible height, the path contents itself with a view of Catstycam, whose fine peak now dominates the scene. Beyond a sheepfold at a confluence, a bridge carries the path over Red Tarn Beck from where the climb begins above its bank. Issuing from the tarn of that name, this lively watercourse guides the path unerringly uphill. A series of zigzags lead to a steadier rise, the restoration of the path easing the way through moister terrain. Ahead, Helvellyn's mighty eastern face appears with Striding Edge gracing the skyline to its left. Towards the top the path runs on to a junction just short of the edge of Red Tarn.

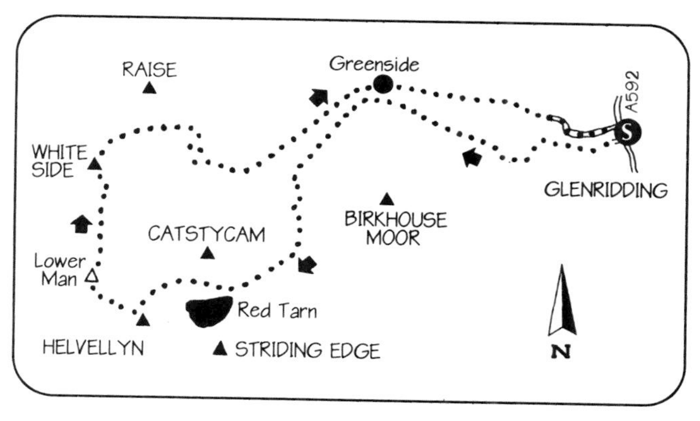

Turn right here, the path quickly rising above the tarn to gain the saddle on Swirral Edge linking Catstycam with Helvellyn. Turning left, the first stage of the edge is a simple near-level walk. At the base of the steep section, an exciting confrontation with Helvellyn's less famous 'edge' begins. Although far shorter than its more illustrious counterpart across the tarn, Swirral Edge has the advantage of a far more solid rock scramble to attain the summit plateau. The only disappointment with Swirral Edge is that it doesn't last long enough.

Those averse to employing hands during the ascent can weave to either side of the arete proper, and the whole episode should only encounter potential danger in winter conditions or very strong winds. From the cairned top a broad path runs left above the escarpment to the Ordnance column, a little beyond which a lacklustre cairn marks the true summit. Just below it is a well patronised shelter.

On a clear day one can finally savour the extensive prospect to the west. Though its two famous edges draw most attention, a contributory factor to Helvellyn's popularity is its reputation as a viewpoint. While not unexpected in view of its altitude, its big advantage is the immense void of central Lakeland to the west, ensuring a lengthy gap before any fells remotely approaching Helvellyn's elevation. As a result the various mountain groups of the district are beheld from a well proportioned distance.

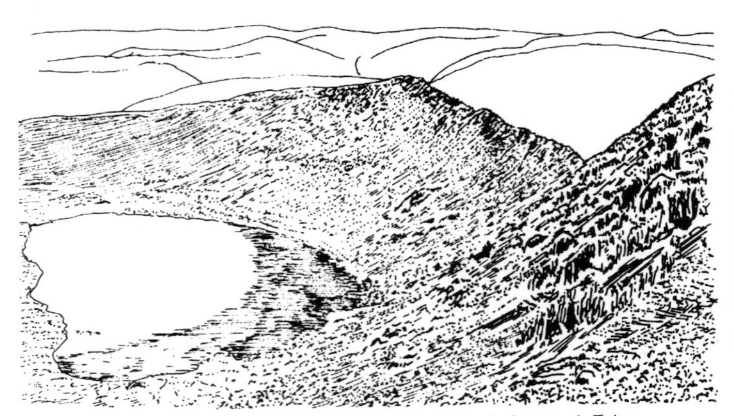

Red Tarn and Striding Edge from the top of Swirral Edge, Helvellyn

From Helvellyn's summit the way lies to the north, and a broad path, much inferior to tracing the escarpment, leaves the OS column, bypassing the top of Swirral Edge and aiming for the lofty saddle in front of Lower Man. Here a broad path forks left for Thirlmere via the top of Browncove Crags, but keep to the ridgetop path. The subsidiary 3000-foot top of Lower Man is breasted before an enjoyable descent of its north rib marks the transfer to less dramatic surroundings, though Catstycam remains superb across Brown Cove. Thirlmere is also well seen down to the left.

Across a col the broad path, choked with cairns, rises to the summit cairn on White Side, the first of a string of rounded tops north of Helvellyn. Though unspectacular in itself, White Side beholds what is possibly an unrivalled grouping of the Helvellyn massif, where to the left of Lower Man (which even manages to look significant) the main summit broods over the twin layers of Swirral and Striding Edges. Pyramidical Catstycam completes the group, its north-west ridge looking positively magnetic.

The path continues down to the next, wider col, with Raise stood beyond. The route, however, now heads for the valley, on the main path which takes a profusely cairned fork right. The path contours across the flank of Raise before slanting downhill, and before long engages a series of broad, lazy zigzags. This was once a popular pony route onto Helvellyn. Catstycam is increasingly impressive across Keppel Cove - note the old concrete dam at the foot of its north-west ridge (see WALK 12). The path drops down to a broad track coming down from Keppel Cove. Turn left on this for a long, steady amble back down towards the Greenside mines, with Sheffield Pike filling the scene ahead.

The track drops down beneath juniper-clad flanks to enter the former mining area. Now a broad stony track, it zigzags down through the upper buildings (now converted for outdoor activities use), crosses Swart Beck and then eases out at the lower buildings, now Helvellyn youth hostel. Beyond here a level stroll on this rough road under Sheffield Pike's flank leads to the terraces of Upper Glenridding, then down the road past the *Travellers Rest* into the village centre.

Helvellyn and Lower Man from the path to the north

14 STYBARROW DODD

SUMMITS
GREEN SIDE 2608ft/795m
STYBARROW DODD 2766ft/843m
RAISE 2897ft/883m

START *Glenridding* ***Grid ref.*** *NY 386169*

DISTANCE *7½ miles/12km* ***ASCENT*** *2840ft/866m*

ORDNANCE SURVEY MAPS
1:50,000 - Landranger 90 *1:25,000 - Outdoor Leisure 5*

ACCESS *Start from the village centre. Large car park. Served by Patterdale-Penrith buses, and seasonal services from Bowness and Keswick.*

A walk over gentle rounded fells high above the lead mining remains of Greenside and the elevated Sticks Pass.

S Leave the village by Greenside Road, on the edge of the car park. This climbs past the *Travellers Rest* to the terraces of Upper Glenridding, then runs a level course as a rough road to the old Greenside lead mines. Passing Helvellyn youth hostel the rough road runs beneath a grassy stabilised bank and crosses Swart Beck to climb between the upper buildings (now converted for outdoor activities use).

Simply keep to the waymarked route for Sticks Pass as the rough and stony track zigzags up past the last buildings and climbs to a fork. The Sticks route rises as a green way to the right, soon enjoying some zigzags to gain height on the juniper-clad flanks. To the left, Catstycam's fine peak dominates the valley of Red Tarn Beck. A long slant to the right runs beneath a crag to rise above the bulk of the spoil heaps. A sharp left turn on this particularly stony section is less clear, but if missed it will quickly be rectified as the cairn sends the side path on to end at a deep, colourful ravine, fronting more old workings.

Just above here the path suddenly becomes an inviting green way. This rises to find a mass of quarry spoil heaps above, with our skyline walk roughly arrayed now, Raise being up to the left. Still well cairned, keep to the path bearing right beneath the spoil, crossing a stream on a simple footbridge then bearing left to the edge of the spoil. Still very intact is the outflow of the abandoned dam of the Sticks Reservoir which served the lead mines. The path runs right alongside the now marshy basin to cairns on a corner at the end.

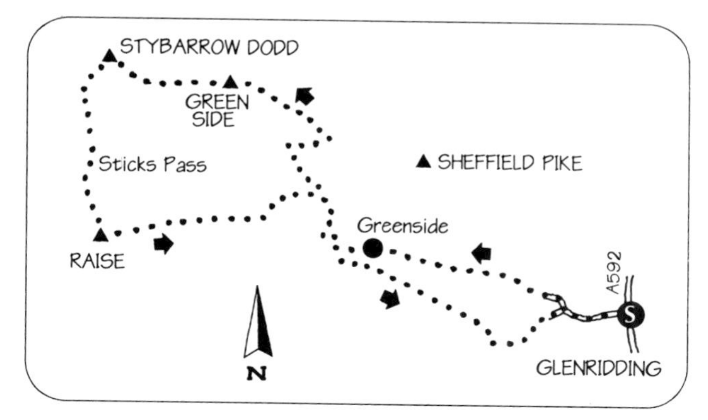

As the Sticks Pass route swings sharp left to run above the marsh, leave it by doubling back to the right, a faint way leading to more spoil beneath a distinctive quarry hole. A green groove leads away, and quickly forks left to rise to a contouring trod beneath a cairn. Turn right on this, curving gently round to the ridgeline above Nick Head. This smashing old way was originally a quarryman's path from Glencoyne. Here it crosses a more modern ascending walkers' path. Turn left up the steep grassy slope of Green Side.

The ascending path avoids some of the steepness by swinging left, rising gently as a well engineered way to arrive on the rim of the great quarry hole beneath which we were recently stood. Don't loiter near the edge in this precarious location. Here the path swings down to the left, so instead simply rise straight up the slope behind the hole, quickly meeting another thin trod on near-level ground above. This rises left to soon reach the broad top of Green Side, marked by a few scattered stones and two cairns, the smaller second one being the summit.

Resume the same way, declining gently before a similar grassy trod climbs onto Stybarrow Dodd's equally broad top. The fading path skirts round to the left of the top, where a cairn is found incorporating an upright slate slab, a boundary stone that formerly stood some distance away. Extensive, rather than exciting views are the order of the day, as will be recounted on the summit of Raise, shortly. The top end of a crumbling wall is found just to the north-east, offering a modicum of shelter if it be needed.

From the cairn drop west to locate the broad ridge-path which also chooses to omit the summit on its journey south from the fellow Dodds. Bear left on this path, which continues along to a cairn on the south-west top. It briefly fades as the way turns south, then re-appears for a rapid descent to the crest of the Sticks Pass. The highest footpass in Lakeland is met amid a peaty interlude, but across it the broad path climbs quickly to the stony summit environs of Raise, with the cairn just to the left. In the great chain of summits stretching north from Helvellyn, Raise heaves itself above its rounded colleagues, and further emphasises its stature with a crown of miniature tors. Though Raise may have no special charisma for fellwalkers, it is better known to winter sports enthusiasts for its ski-tow and hut.

The smelt mill chimney on Stang, looking to Sheffield Pike

With modern English winters providing much frustration for the ski brigade, they might well aspire to gain the mountain's summit to enjoy the splendid panorama, snow or no snow. There are few omissions from this star-studded cast, with the team award going to the elegant outlines of the Grasmoor group, supported by individual performances from the masses of Skiddaw and Blencathra. Crystal clear winter days bring views beyond the confines of Lakeland to Cross Fell and its satellites in the North Pennines; Ingleborough 40 miles further south; and even an array of Scottish hills across the Solway Firth.

Though the Helvellyn skyline beckons to the south, instead head ea a pathless walk which within a minute reveals the Stang chimney anc flue on a grassy shelf below. Far below that are Glenridding and the head of Ullswater. Simply descend the easy slopes past a rash of stones supporting a rock tor, with the top of the ski tow to the left. The remains of the chimney are quickly reached, and from this vicinity Catstycam and Helvellyn form an impressive picture.

The stone-arched flue carried poisonous fumes away from the mine to the chimney, a rare sight in Lakeland but a common feature on many a Pennine hillside. From here the line of the collapsed flue leads unfailingly down, swinging sharply left towards the bottom to drop down onto the outward route directly above the steep drop to the Greenside mines. Retrace steps back to Glenridding, ideally using the following variation finish.

For variety, on entering the site just below the Keppelcove fork, a waymark sends you right, down to a track above Red Tarn Beck. Just a minute upstream is a footbridge, and from the path on its other side turn left for a pleasanter return high above the Glenridding valley. Ultimately it arrives at a gate/stile off the fell, and drops down through a pasture and down past Mires Beck Farm, crossing Rattlebeck Bridge to rejoin Greenside Road on the edge of the village.

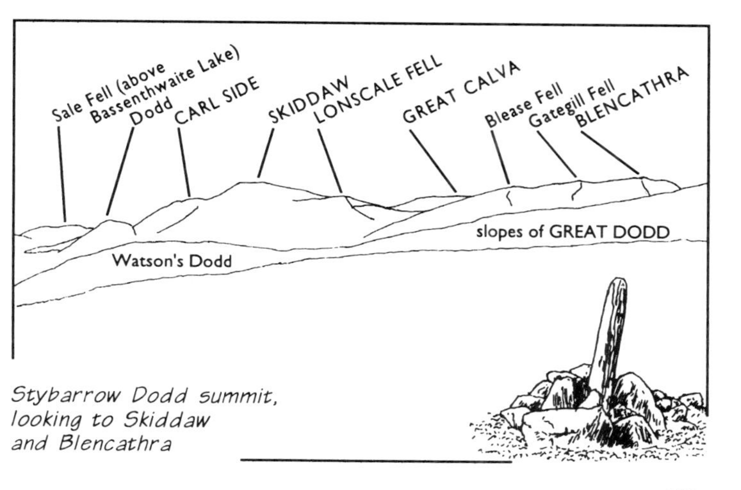

Stybarrow Dodd summit, looking to Skiddaw and Blencathra

SWINESIDE KNOTT

SUMMITS
SWINESIDE KNOTT 1814ft/553m

START *Park Brow, Ullswater* ***Grid ref.*** *NY 397205*

DISTANCE *4½ miles/7km* ***ASCENT*** *1296ft/395m*

ORDNANCE SURVEY MAPS
1:50,000 - Landranger 90 *1:25,000 - Outdoor Leisure 5*

ACCESS *Start from an unsigned car park on the A5091 (east side), between Dockray and Ullswater. Alternative starts are the National Trust's Aira Force car park at the junction with the A592 (this adds on an extra half-mile); or from Dockray, which is on the route. Served by seasonal Keswick-Patterdale buses. The A592 alongside Ullswater is served by Penrith-Patterdale buses.*

An undemanding fellwalk with outstanding views over Ullswater, from some excellent paths made by lead miners bound for the Greenside mines in the upper Glenridding valley. Largely off the beaten track, other than the memorable brush with Aira Force.

S From the car park cross the road to a stile, and bear left along a thin path through the scattered trees of Glencoyne Park. This path sets our course for the opening 1½ miles, the first mile of which remains largely level as it charts a course along the bracken-clad lower flanks of Watermillock Common. With very little height gained, all thoughts can turn to the constantly improving view over the upper half of Ullswater backed by an exceptional ring of fells. Directly ahead, meanwhile, is the distinguished knoll of Swineside Knott.

After a couple of clusters of trees the path finally makes an effort to gain more height, enjoying a slant across to a sturdy descending wall. Over the stile the path climbs above a gnarled beechwood and finally makes its first change of direction, a brief zigzag to beat the steep contours. This is perhaps the finest viewpoint, looking down on

GOWBARROW FELL

SUMMITS
GOWBARROW FELL 1578ft/481m

START *Park Brow, Ullswater* ***Grid ref.*** *NY 400200*

DISTANCE *4½ miles/7km* ***ASCENT*** *1100ft/335m*

ORDNANCE SURVEY MAPS
1:50,000 - Landranger 90 *1:25,000 - Outdoor Leisure 5*

ACCESS *Start from the National Trust's Aira Force car park on the A592 Penrith-Patterdale road at Park Brow Foot, near the junction with the A5091. Served by Penrith-Patterdale buses and seasonal Patterdale-Keswick buses.*

Gowbarrow Fell is the last concentration of real fell country in the north-east of the district, and it manages to boast two outstanding features. The first is Aira Force, a truly beautiful and highly accessible waterfall below its western slopes, the second is its panoramic pictures of Ullswater.

S The popular Aira Force car park features tearooms, toilets and an information point. Leave by the bustling path at its far end, which soon dives into the trees. Bear right shortly after on the path down to a wooden footbridge over Aira Beck, and keep right when the path up the other side forks. A little further, the waterfall traffic can be escaped completely by bearing right again to a stile in a fence onto the open fell, just beyond which another clear path heads along to the right.

Running briefly along the base of Gowbarrow Fell, with Ullswater down to the right, another fork is soon reached. Take the inviting path slanting up to the left, which provides a steady means of gaining height while also extending the outstanding views over the lake. Individual features of note include the novel shape of the former shooting lodge of Lyulph's Tower immediately below; and the little settlement of Sandwick midway along the opposite shore. The path soon levels out and contours along the southern flank of the fell, ignoring a rougher branch climbing left part way on. Arrival at a distinct corner by a memorial seat of 1905 marks one of the walk's many highlights. A stile on the right gives access to a prominent cairn high above Yew Crag: a firm grip should be kept on young children! The head of Ullswater with its gallery of mountains is seen to perfection as illustrated overleaf, while the less frequented Martindale Fells are superbly arrayed directly across the lake.

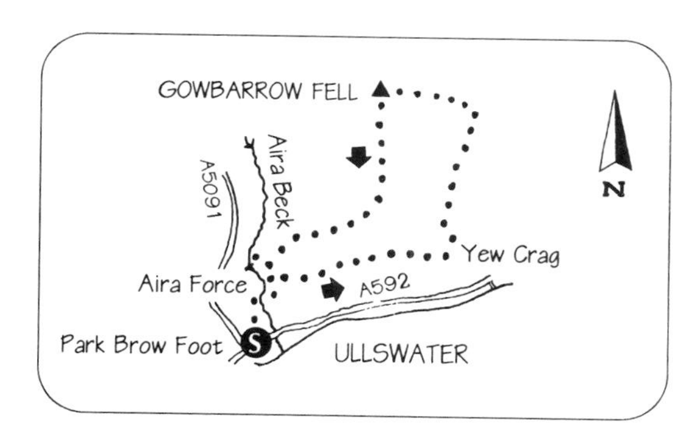

From here the path swings around to the left and maintains its undemanding course, rising ever gently as it traverses the fell's eastern flank, again in grand style. This section ends at a decaying shooting box just before a wall, where the path leaves Gowbarrow for the plantations of Swinburn's Park. Ignoring the stile, our route turns up to the left on a path rising above the wall and a tiny beck, passing gradually from bracken to heather (a more direct path rises from the ruin, but encounters marshier ground and is generally less appealing). A little damp higher up, the path concludes with a pull to the left to gain the distinct summit of the fell. An Ordnance Survey column adorned with a National Trust sign doubly confirms the location.

While the fells around Blencathra to the north-west and the Martindale district across the lake are well seen, the intimate picture of the lake itself is not available from this location. To rectify this, turn south along the broad, heathery and occasionally marshy ridge on the left-hand of two clear paths. As grassier terrain takes over, a better path forms to run along to a conspicuous cairn on Green Hill, which appears well in advance, almost at the ridge-end. Here a pleasant discovery is made in the shape of an inviting green path, which turns to the right to take us down in precisely the direction required. The whole descent is a total joy, the view of the upper reaches of the lake backed by the mighty Helvellyn range matching the quality of the path underfoot.

At the bottom a fence is reached, and just along to the left is a gate only yards from the stile where we first gained the fellside. To complete the walk in the appropriate manner, turn right along the path to Aira Force. Just before the waterfall it forks to provide an opportunity to view the spectacle from a tiny arched bridge above. This bears a tablet touchingly inscribed *Stephen Edward Spring Rice CB 1856 - 1902. He would have liked his brother Gerald, who 14 years after him also gave his life for his country, to be commemorated on this spot.* Return down the path to the bridge at the foot of the fall for the more conventional view (illustrated on page 61). The lower path heading back downstream can now be taken to return to the bridge at the outset of the walk, retracing the first steps back to the car park.

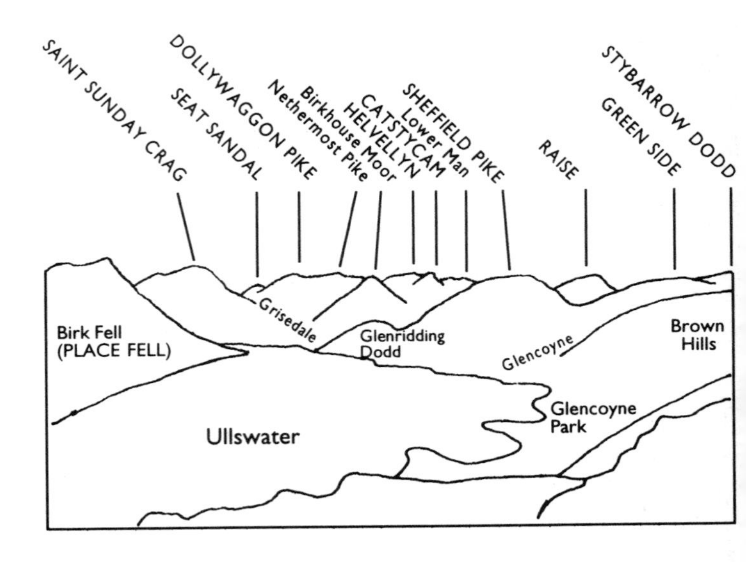

Above and Opposite:
The head of Ullswater from above Yew Crag

17 GREAT DODD

SUMMITS	
CLOUGH HEAD	*2382ft/726m*
GREAT DODD	*2812ft/857m*

START *Dockray* ***Grid ref.*** *NY 380219*

DISTANCE *8½ miles/13½km* ***ASCENT*** *1985ft/605m*

ORDNANCE SURVEY MAPS
1:50,000 - Landranger 90 *1:25,000 - Outdoor Leisure 5*

ACCESS *Start from the minor crossroads at High Row, less than a mile west of the A5091 at Dockray. Ample parking. Dockray is served by seasonal Keswick-Patterdale buses.*

Easy walking on grassy fells: a stress-free outing away from the crowds.

S Leave the crossroads by the only unsurfaced branch, that going west through a gate at a sheepfold at the plantation corner. This is the Old Coach Road, an historic route between St. John's in the Vale and Dockray. It is superbly engineered and charts a well graded and infallible course around the northern base of the Dodds ridge. On leaving the plantation the road makes a sharp turn at the crossing of Groove Beck, the point to which the walk will return. Beyond here the appearance of Blencathra more than compensates for a second section of plantation which briefly shadows us.

Clough Head appears straight ahead as the way fully opens out: Skiddaw and its tops have joined Blencathra across the wastes of Barbaryrigg Moss, while Wolf Crags look down on our route from the left. Enjoy a good stride out as the road swings away from the fellside to cross the grassy hummocks of Barbary Rigg (a glacial moraine). The old road passes Barbaryrigg Fold then drops to cross the exit from Wolfcrag Moss, with the knob of Calfhow Pike, between the walk's two summits, prominent up the side valley of Mosedale.

At Mariel Bridge Mosedale Beck is crossed, and looking upstream Great Dodd itself is the great bulk up above. By now Clough Head's summit has dropped back to allow the minor top of White Pike to take precedence. Ignoring the first stile in the accompanying fence, forge on up the old road to reach another stile on a brow. White Pike makes a prominent objective directly above, so across the stile enjoy a pathless grassy climb to its cairn, the final steeper stage being through the pleasant stony slopes. A large cairn crowns a rash of boulders, with a view down to the village of Threlkeld sheltering under Blencathra.

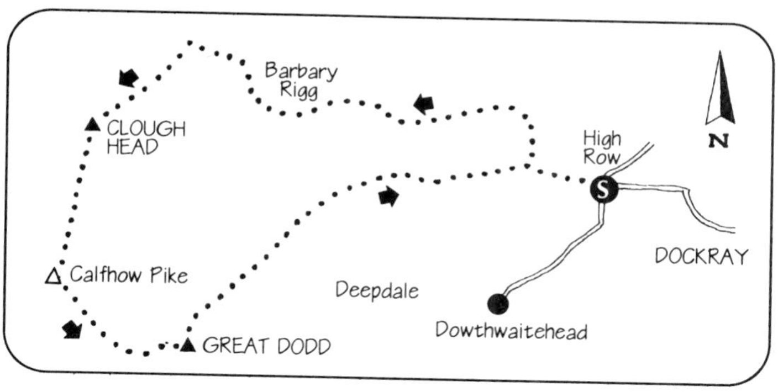

Resume up the grassy slope behind, a faint trod guiding the way to a sudden arrival on a steeply plunging edge. This gives great depth to the first views to the west, as a gentle rise left quickly reveals the summit. Helvellyn and its Lower Man appear just before reaching the Ordnance Survey column and shelter. Clough Head is the northern outpost of the Helvellyn range, and the ultimate reward is found in two major aspects of the view. Firstly the prospect of Blencathra, a classic mountain study, while westwards is a succession of delights, with the Vale of Keswick featuring both Bassenthwaite Lake and Derwentwater. The foot of the latter is backed by the shapely outlines of the Grasmoor group, while continuing further round, Scafell Pike and its considerable supporting cast acquit themselves admirably.

Turning away, the dome of Great Dodd fills the ridge, and a path heads southwards to immediately reveal Thirlmere below. This grassy stroll gives ample opportunity to savour the western panorama before reaching Calfhow Pike just across the saddle. This solid tor makes an intriguing halfway point, sitting uneasily in its grassy surround. The climb to Great Dodd is uneventful, a steady pull at the top of which the path fades on the final steeper section. Continue up to find the summit cairn sat alone on the broad domed top. A useful shelter stands 150 yards to its south-east.

This fell of immense girth displays few distinguishing features, and in common with its fellow Dodds is territory for the walker who prefers long strides and distant horizons. The two contrasting panoramas are of a succession of ridges westwards, and eastwards the unbroken chain of Pennine heights, far beyond the sprawl of no-man's-land marking the boundary of this corner of Lakeland.

Wolf Crags from Mariel Bridge

Leave by heading briefly north, and though initially bare, a good path quickly forms as you curve round to the north-east. This descends onto the Randerside plateau, where a cairn has been fashioned from the outcrops on its crest. The path curves beneath it to resume the descent amid a landscape essentially Pennine in character. Very easy strides lead down gentle slopes, interrupted by a marshy plateau on the edge of Whams Moss. This is soon escaped as the path returns to pristine condition for a superb grassy stride above the marshy environs of Groove Beck. The path descends at the end to rejoin the outward route alongside Groovebeck Fold. Turn right on the Old Coach Road to be finished within minutes.

Skiddaw and Lonscale Fell from the Coach Road

18 PLACE FELL

SUMMITS
BIRK FELL 1680ft/512m
PLACE FELL 2155ft/657m

START *Sandwick* ***Grid ref.*** *NY 423195*

DISTANCE *5½ miles/9km* ***ASCENT*** *1900ft/579m*

ORDNANCE SURVEY MAPS
1:50,000 - Landranger 90 *1:25,000 - Outdoor Leisure 5*

ACCESS *Start from the unfenced road just before it drops down to end at Sandwick. Limited verge parking. An option is to park a car on Martindale Hause, and follow the path to Sandwick by way of Hallin Bank and Bridge End. Served by Postbus from Penrith.*

Few mountains in Lakeland have better defined boundaries than Place Fell, a splendid self-contained package of colourful upland. Though most ascents emanate from Patterdale, unquestionably more rewarding is the climb from Sandwick, making the most of the two broad ridges leaving the felltop.

S Just above the handful of buildings at Sandwick the walk starts on the wide track heading west along the foot of the open fell, bound for Patterdale. Ahead, the prominent beacon on Low Birk Fell is the finest of several tops and knolls above the bracken flanks, and is our first objective. The popular path is vacated before it gains Ullswater's shore, and the break comes after crossing a bridge over lively Scalehow Beck, whose waterfalls will have already aroused interest. After the short rise to the wall corner beyond the bridge, a thinner path runs through bracken on the left, soon climbing a little to draw level with Scalehow Force.

Just above the upper waterslide the path fades, and the object is to gain the low ridge up to the right, emanating from Low Birk Fell. Briefly climb through bracken to low outcrops on the right, then work across a little further to locate a tenuous trod that climbs enjoyably between the minor outcrops of the well-defined ridge end. Over to the left the broad summit rises above the beginnings of Scalehow Beck, with the contrastingly shapely profile of the Knight to its right. With Ullswater far below, this section soon terminates at the splendidly sited beacon on Low Birk Fell. This is a good place to take stock, as the upland stage of the climb can be surveyed with the curving arm of Birk Fell connecting with the higher ground of the summit. There is also a grand appearance of the high Helvellyn massif.

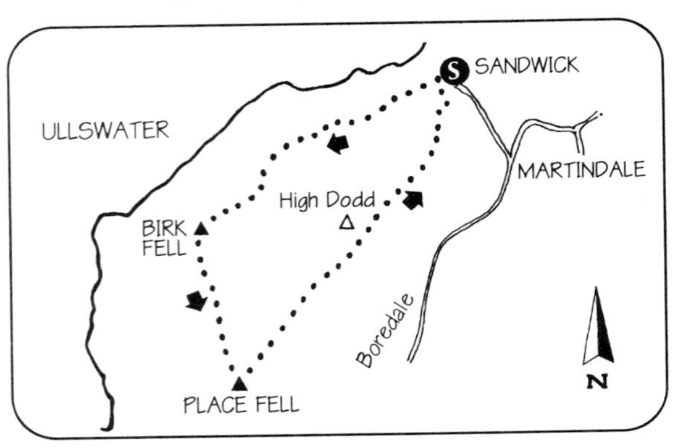

A delectable trod now sets forth over the ridge's grassy undulations, then curving up to the left past twin ruins. The trod diminishes further to reach the base of a short, steep climb onto Birk Fell proper, with views down the steep and colourful western flank to Ullswater. A cairn offers a greeting on the crest of the ridge, but the real top is set further back to the right, marked by a scrappy cairn. This proves to be a splendid top, with an absolutely glorious prospect over the lake to the Helvellyn range featuring Catstycam. Also particularly notable are the resplendent pairings of Sheffield Pike and Glencoyne; Birkhouse Moor and Glenridding; and Saint Sunday Crag and Grisedale.

A faint trod descends to a marshy depression, which is best skirted to the right, earning a prolonged bonus of the Ullswater scene. Across the marsh, a direct climb from Ullswater gains the fell by way of a groove, and united, the two ways form a clearer green path making for the summit. Rising behind the cairned top of the Knight (which makes a short and worthwhile detour), the path becomes clearer still for the final short pull. The top is an extensive place in keeping with its all-round openness, but an elevated rocky platform makes for an unmistakeable summit, with an Ordnance Survey column inspirationally sited atop a craggy little face. The absence of intervening higher ground ensures a first-class panorama, with the Kirkstone and High Street fells and ridges particularly well arrayed.

Two major paths depart the summit, one south to Boredale Hause, the other north-east past a tarn. This is the way to Sandwick, along the crest of Hart Crag and descending pleasantly to an old sheepfold on Low Moss. A clear path bearing left after the fold provides the quickest and easiest way down, but in good weather higher ground can be savoured as long as possible by remaining on the inviting path straight ahead. As it swings round beneath the grassy alp of High Dodd up to the left, this delectable green swathe offers another exit to the valley, in the form of a superlative path winding down through bracken on the right.

Where the path sets off for the valley, the ridge can be used still longer by continuing on, the broad path soon becoming a thin trod after the junction. It maintains this fashion on the grassy ridge top of Sleet Fell to terminate abruptly at a substantial cairn above a sudden drop to Howe Grain. Here go left with a well collapsed wall, which sets the course for the last stage of the descent. While one can simply follow the course of the old wall down to meet a path linking Low Moss and Sandwick, an alternative path quickly veers right, away from the wall. This is soon deflected left by steeper ground, with Sandwick appearing below. This final stage offers yet more superb views as the bracken zone is entered. The path becomes a broad green way, zigzagging down to the base of the fell just above the start.

Ullswater and Hallin Fell from Low Birk Fell

19 BEDA FELL

SUMMITS
BEDA FELL 1670ft/509m

START *Martindale* **Grid ref.** *NY 434183*

DISTANCE *5 miles/8km* **ASCENT** *1250ft/381m*

ORDNANCE SURVEY MAPS
1:50,000 - Landranger 90 1:25,000 - Outdoor Leisure 5

ACCESS *Start from Martindale Old Church, on the far side of Martindale Hause from Howtown. Limited roadside parking. Served by Postbus from Penrith. Howtown is served by steamer (seasonal) from Glenridding and Pooley Bridge.*

A prominent feature in the celebrated Martindale landscape, Beda Fell offers a fascinating climb, an undemanding grassy ridge, and a rewarding picture of the north-eastern quadrant of Lakeland.

S From St. Martin's church cross Christy Bridge over Howe Grain Beck and then leave the road by turning up the fellside by Winter Crag Farm. Already Beda Fell is underfoot, and the path to take is a slowly forming one climbing with a crumbling wall on the right, in preference to the more obvious green track running along behind the farm. Within minutes the path rises above the wall, and at the gentlest of angles gains Beda Fell's ridge at a green crossroads. The surprise of an iron seat awaits, tempting an early break to savour the first view of Ullswater backed by Gowbarrow Fell. The steep flanks of Place Fell line Boredale, to the west.

Turn left to commence the ascent proper, and almost immediately the path confronts the finest feature of the ridge, the knobbly crest of Winter Crag. The path narrowly skirts the rocky top, from where Beda Fell's summit is seen behind a prominent cairn. The path now settles down to a steady climb, with lovely views into the side valleys of Bannerdale and Boredale. As more height is gained the previously glimpsed prominent cairn is reached, with the summit cairn waiting across a small depression. The summit of the fell is actually known as Beda Head, the name deriving from St. Bede.

Pleasing features of the view are the Hallin Fell area with Ullswater stretching away behind, and the high peaks encircling Grisedale appearing over the gap of Boredale Hause. Of the many charming aspects of the Martindale area, the prospect of the Nab, in the heart of the secluded deer forest, is as fair as any. Just slotting into place is the church where the walk began.

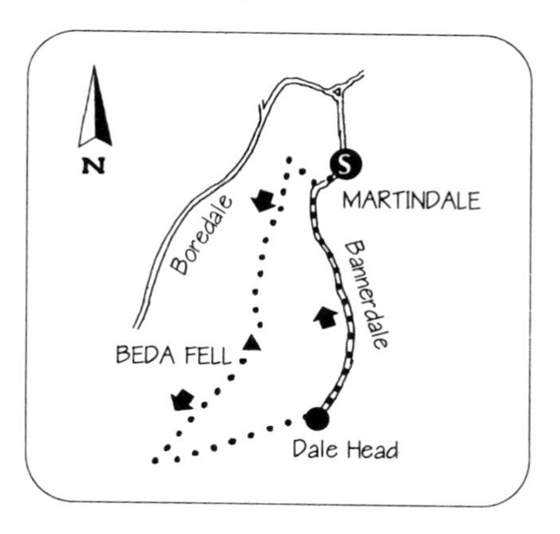

Having climbed to this altitude there is now no urgency to lose it, and the path heads off along the grassy ridge-top. After a marshy beginning the path settles down to a relaxing, undulating trod, with Heck Crag and Angletarn Pikes occupying the ridge farther on. Well before these heights, however, the ridge is to be vacated by means of a transverse path, an old packhorse route linking Bannerdale and Boredale Hause.

A little surprisingly the path does not cross the ridge at its lowest point, in the usual manner, but a short way up the other side. Having barely gained any appreciable height beyond the lowest point, the ridge path comes up against the rocky bluff of Bedafell Knott. Here a slimmer path cleverly evades the short pull by contouring left to join the aforementioned return path, which can be seen from this point. True followers of good paths will scale Bedafell Knott, passing its cairned top to run on to the path crossroads, marked by another cairn.

Vacate the ridge by doubling sharply back to the left, and the old way immediately commences a superlative descent towards Bannerdale. At a roofless stone hut the short-cut path comes in: glance back uphill to appraise the route's classic engineered course. A broad, slanting and delectable green way leads down through the bracken to meet the intake wall just short of Dale Head.

Behind the farm buildings, a branch left avoids the yard by dropping to a plank footbridge, then down to a stile and bridle-gate. Here a surfaced road takes over, and its traffic-free course is followed back to the church through the valley of Howe Grain in deepest Martindale. En route the road passes the old deer skinning shed on the right, with its giveaway chimneys, while on the left Beda Fell's craggy flank features the impressive buttress of Raven Crag high above the farm at Thrang Crag.

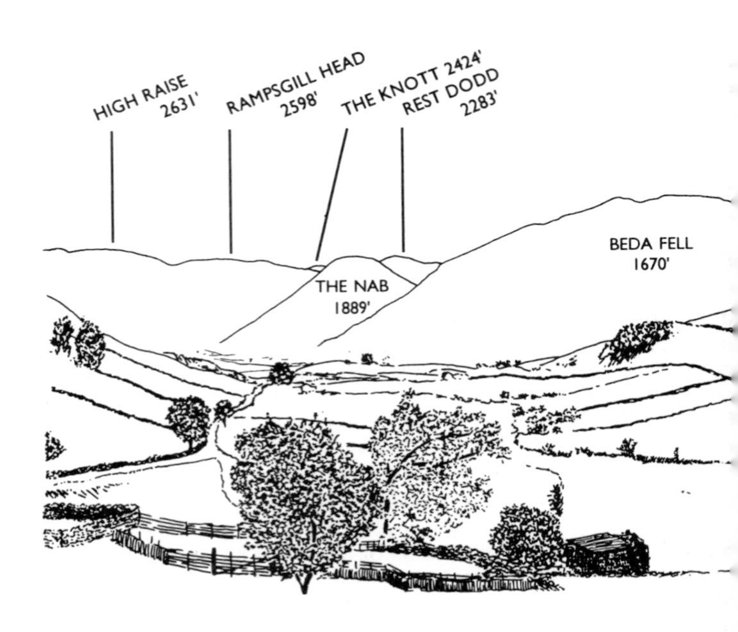

Beda Fell and the Martindale skyline from near Martindale Hause

Saint Sunday Crag skyline behind. At an early fork remai
path which swings down to the right. Encountering a peat
it then runs on more pleasantly in the company of a wall an
contouring round to the colourful crest of Satura Crag. Our re
valley of Bannerdale is well seen down to the right.

On Satura Crag the wall returns for company until arrival at a gate, then the path continues around the grassy alp above Buck Crag, once again overlooking Bannerdale. Angle Tarn is quickly revealed just ahead, and the path drops down to its shore. With its indented bays this delightful sheet of water makes a charming foreground to the skyline of high fells across the hidden Patterdale valley (see illustrations on pages 28 and 34).

When level with the main island abandon the broad highway by crossing over the low grassy saddle on the right, and a thin path will be located turning down to the left in the company of the sturdy wall enclosing the deer forest at the head of Bannerdale. After a spell by the wall the path breaks off for an exhilarating traverse beneath Heck Crag, rejoining the wall once the rougher environs subside.

Departure from this magnificent valley head is along a gem of a green path through bracken, merging into a broader green way to arrive at the farm of Dale Head. A branch left to a bridle-gate avoids the yard. Here a surfaced road takes over, and its traffic-free course is followed back to the church through the valley of Howe Grain in deepest Martindale. The last half-mile has the craggy flank of Beda Fell up to the left, and also passes the old deer skinning shed, with its giveaway chimneys.

Looking down Bannerdale from Satura Crag, with Beda Fell on the left and Bonscale Pike at the back

BONSCALE PIKE

SUMMITS	
ARTHUR'S PIKE	1745ft/532m
BONSCALE PIKE	1719ft/524m

START *Howtown* **Grid ref.** *NY 444198*

DISTANCE *7 miles/11km* **ASCENT** *1450ft/442m*

ORDNANCE SURVEY MAPS
1:50,000 - Landranger 90 *1:25,000 - Outdoor Leisure 5*

ACCESS *Start from the Howtown Hotel. Limited parking at the foot of Martindale Hause, a little further on the road. The hotel has a patron's car park, but ideally, in season, come in style by motor launch from Glenridding or Pooley Bridge. Served by Postbus from Penrith.*

The twin buttresses of Arthur's Pike and Bonscale Pike boldly overlook the lower reach of Ullswater, yet their ascent proves to be the gentlest in the book.

S From the hotel, which cannot be missed as there is little else at Howtown, head up the access road to its left, rising with Fusedale Beck to emerge into open country at the entrance to Fusedale. Turn immediately down to the left to a stone slab footbridge on the beck. From it rise to a stile onto the drive of Mellguards. A gate straight ahead, between the two houses, gives access to the foot of the steep flank of Bonscale Pike.

That slope is for the descent however, and reassuringly for now the broad green path to the left is the way to go. Curving right and rising gently it remains in the company of the intake wall for a considerable time, during which it shows little intention to gain any appreciable height. Aside from the permanent views over Ullswater, the highlight is passing below the magnificent ravine of Swarthbeck Gill, which divides the two objectives of the walk.

Eventually the main path leaves the wall to commence a delectable, supremely engineered climb. Ahead, the wooded Dunmallard Hill overlooks the foot of the lake; behind is Penrith overlooked by Beacon Edge, while the North Pennines fill the skyline beyond, across the Eden Valley. The green path slants boldly up through bracken towards a wall corner enclosing the woodland of Barton Park. For an extension to visit the Cockpit stone circle, see the panel overleaf. Just short of the wall the main route takes a thinner branch right, which swings more sharply uphill to curve up to the skyline just beyond the outcrop of White Knott. At any stage one is likely to come across some of the ponies that graze semi-wild on these moorland slopes.

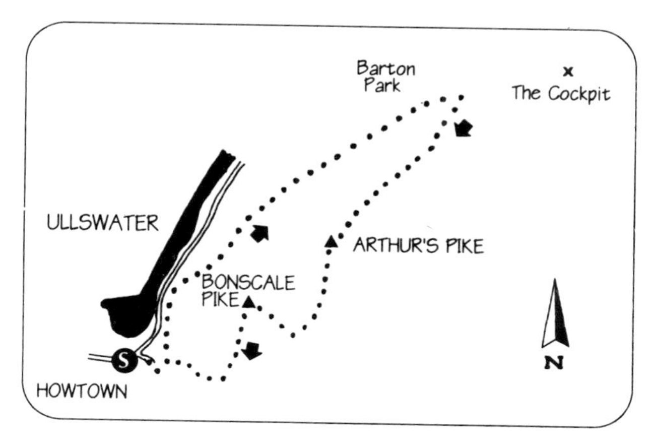

A slim path doubles back to steadily gain height on this wide shoulder above Arthur's Pike's steepening northern face. Look back over the plateau of Moor Divock to survey a greatly extended Pennine skyline. A cairn on White Knott is gained, and the modestly worn way remains clear along the edge of a steeper drop. When the path forks each aims for a skyline cairn, and the left one steers a more direct course for the summit. More rewarding, however, is the right one, which remains truer to the edge, where rolling grass gives way to craggy declivities.

The felltop appears on gaining either of these cairns, and from the right one a trod runs on to the final 'edge' cairn to enjoy a detailed study of Ullswater and its environs. The lower reach is seen as on a map, wrapped between tidy parcels of hedgerowed fields. Looking up the gun barrel into the higher fell country, meanwhile, the lake is seen at its best, in a deep basin of mountains backed by the great wall of Helvellyn. From this final cairn a fine pyramidical specimen crowns a much steeper drop just below. As the path finally expires here, simply rise left for 200 yards to the cairn marking the summit of Arthur's Pike. With its ally Bonscale Pike, Arthur's Pike mounts an exceedingly impressive display of rough fellside above the strip of green pastures by the lower reach of Ullswater. From almost all other quarters the fell is seen in true perspective, as a cornerstone of the lofty High Street range.

Bonscale Pike's crest is clearly in view from Arthur's Pike, though intervening Swarthbeck Gill necessitates a detour to avoid losing undue height. Begin by turning south-east to cross the marshy plateau for 100 yards to gain a good track, following it right for 150 yards to a crossroads. The right arm gravitates towards the upper reaches of Swarth Beck, slanting down to an old sheepfold by the beck. Cross the stream here and slant half-right to Bonscale Pike's grassy top.

Looking up Ullswater from Bonscale Pike

In common with Arthur's Pike, Bonscale Pike is no more than a buttress of the extensive High Street range, for behind its anonymous top, dull slopes begin an immediate rise to Loadpot Hill. To appreciate the fell's finer points stroll a few yards north from the scrappy cairn, where an assortment of stone men cluster above the steep drop. These splendid pillars frame a stunning picture of Ullswater, making this very much a place to linger. The westernmost pillar perches on a craggy knoll and offers a bird's-eye view of Howtown and the little bay of Howtown Wyke backed by Hallin Fell.

The return to Howtown begins by turning south on a slender, contouring path above the steep drop. Glorious views now sweep up into the heart of the lonely fell country of Martindale, and can be relished for the remainder of the walk. Only a little height is lost as the trod runs on to approach the first beck cutting down the fellside. On turning down by its dry course an improved path materialises, and is soon zigzagging down the unremitting flank in skilfully constructed fashion. Before long it forsakes the beck and works its green way down towards the prominent houses at Mellguards, finishing a little more steeply to rejoin the outward route at the gate off the fell.

Either finish the walk as it began, or once back on the road in Fusedale, climb the slope behind to find a broad path running along the wallside. This leads around the hollow of the Coombs to Martindale Hause, but if wishing to return to the foot of the pass, simply break off when the wall does to cross to meet the road.

The Cockpit stone circle is surprisingly extensive, consisting of a largely unbroken chain of stones on what is virtually a plateau on the moor. It is most likely a burial site dating from the Bronze Age, and was certainly here long before the Romans strode out along the nearby High Street. For a detour to visit the Cockpit, keep straight on the ascending path above Barton Park, tracing the wall to the deep confines of Aik Beck. Across it, keep straight on the broad track which leads within a few minutes to the circle, at a crossroads of ways. Rejoin the route by re-crossing Aik Beck, then take the green way slanting up to the left: leave this shortly to find the fainter way of the main route on the initially grassy edge that forms.

The Cockpit stone circle

23 HIGH STREET

SUMMITS	
ROUGH CRAG	*2060ft/628m*
HIGH STREET	*2717ft/828m*
KIDSTY PIKE	*2559ft/780m*

START *Mardale Head* ***Grid ref.*** *NY 469107*

DISTANCE *7 miles/11km* ***ASCENT*** *2360ft/720m*

ORDNANCE SURVEY MAPS
1:50,000 - Landranger 90 *1:25,000 - Outdoor Leisure 5*

ACCESS *Start from the road end car park at the head of Haweswater. Buses from Penrith at weekends and Bank Holidays, May to August.*

Highest mountain east of the Kirkstone Pass, High Street is invariably ascended as focal point of a longer walk around the Martindale or Kentmere fells. However, by far its finest aspect and approach are from the east, where a rugged ridge climbs impressively from valley to summit plateau. The possibility of witnessing the magnificent spectacle of England's only nesting Golden Eagles (whose eyrie is close throughout this walk) is a further attraction.

S From the car park take the broad path heading away, within a couple of minutes forking at a wall corner. Turn right on the wallside path, descending to cross Mardale Beck flowing into the head of Haweswater, then doubling back alongside the slender upper finger of the reservoir. The wooded spur of the Rigg, ahead, cloaks the foot of the object ridge, and as the path rises towards the wall and plantation at its brow, a grassy path turns into the bracken to commence a stirring ascent.

In the company of the old wall the path remains clear throughout, and the surroundings increase in grandeur as height is gained. At an early grassy saddle, a gap in the wall offers a first true appraisal of the Riggindale scene. The path keeps to the south of the initially craggy crest, but ultimately gains it to enjoy views across Riggindale to the peak of Kidsty Pike, final summit of the walk. Becoming broader, gentler and grassier, Rough Crag's summit appears in front, backed by the powerful wall of its parent fell. A short, steeper pull could almost be fashioned into a simple scramble, then it's a short walk to the rocky summit.

Ahead is the great wall of High Street, while below are the sombre waters of Blea Water's circular pool. The path descends to a col, Caspel Gate, from where an easy escape route drops left down the grassy slope to Blea Water. The ascent resumes less steeply than anticipated, the situation being dramatic without being unnerving. Suddenly the path emerges onto a contrastingly spacious plateau. High Street's summit lies to the south-west, and a wall traversing it from north to south ensures it is soon found.

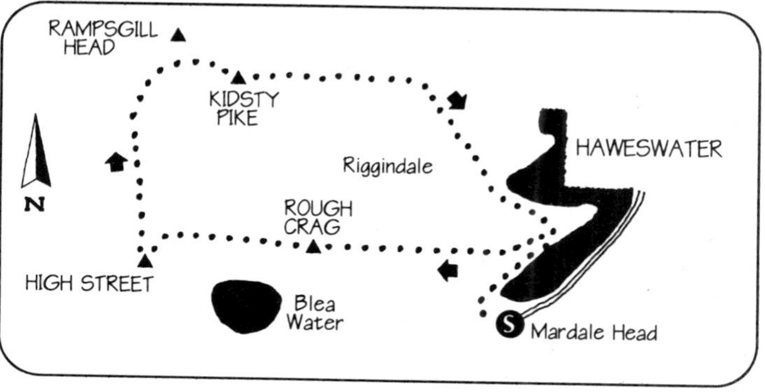

For those with a sense of history, High Street offers a Roman road - hence the name - and the location of occasional horse races, again recalled in today's little known alternative name, Racecourse Hill. The greater fame stems from its adoption by those indomitable Romans for the creation of their 'highway in the sky', to link forts at Ambleside and Brougham.

Marked by an Ordnance column, a crumbling wall and two sprawling piles of stones, the summit is a bleak and barren place, and while Roman legions may have marched over it and horses raced across it, there is little excitement today. The view, similarly, is extensive rather than interesting, with a panorama stretching from Coniston Old Man to Blencathra.

Heading north, there is a choice of routes to the saddle known as the Straits of Riggindale. Easiest option simply follows the wall, alternatively drop west to quickly find the broad course of the Roman road (good views down into Hayeswater); or return to trace the edge over the cairned knoll of Short Stile. The Roman road passes through the wall in the neat saddle, then rises up the other side. Very quickly, however, it forks right at a cairn to keep the route faithful to the steep rim of Riggindale, passing above Twopenny Crag. Though the old highway bears off left indiscernibly, the well trodden modern highway clings to the edge to curve round to the waiting peak of Kidsty Pike.

Kidsty Pike's impressive profile masks the fact that it is merely a minor upthrust on the shoulder of Rampsgill Head, but its spectacular drop into Riggindale is no sham, nor its position for appraising the route thus far. Across the depths of Riggindale the knobbly crest of Rough Crag climbs to the great ridge of High Street, whose forbidding crags and shattered rocks form a majestic spectacle. The captive waters of Mardale lap the fellside far below, with an extensive Pennine skyline far beyond.

The descent begins on a briefly faint path which within yards becomes clear, to enjoy an uncomplicated return to the valley. Two easy grassy sections are split by the rougher interruption of the outcrops of Kidsty Howes. Throughout the descent, Haweswater waits patiently below. Towards the bottom the path drops to a stone footbridge on lively Randale Beck. Don't cross, but turn right on the path to cross Rannerdale Beck, instead, just yards from the lakeshore. The path runs on past the RSPB observation hut and through a stand of larch, then slants up old pastures to regain the foot of the Rigg, alongside the plantations. Ahead, the final stage awaits, and Harter Fell dominates this last half-mile as the path returns past the upper finger of the lake back to the road end.

Summit cairn,
Kidsty Pike

24 BRANSTREE

SUMMITS	
SELSIDE PIKE	*2149ft/655m*
BRANSTREE	*2339ft/713m*

START *Mardale Head* ***Grid ref.*** *NY 469107*

DISTANCE *6 miles/9½km* ***ASCENT*** *1650ft/503m*

ORDNANCE SURVEY MAPS
1:50,000 - Landranger 90 *1:25,000 - Outdoor Leisure 5*

ACCESS *Start from the road end car park at the head of Haweswater. Buses from Penrith at weekends and Bank Holidays, May to August.*

A magnificent historic route offers an easy leg-up onto two unfrequented summits at the head of Mardale. An easy bonus is available with the option to add Harter Fell to the day's outing.

S Unlike all the other walkers, leave the car park by heading back along the road for a mile: in fact, a permissive path leaves a stile at the car park entrance to take a lakeside route, a little untidy in parts but at least it's off the road. The road is left shortly after it bridges Hopgill Beck. If on the path, the beck is crossed by a neat stone arched footbridge, after which branch right on a path up to a gate back onto the road. Either way, the views from the outset are great, looking across the lake to Harter Fell, High Street and Kidsty Pike.

Virtually opposite, a gate sends a green path rising away. This is the old Corpse Road, the route by which the folk of Mardale took their dead for burial at Shap, prior to having their own church. Cruelly, the community of Mardale has itself been history since the valley was drowned by Manchester Corporation in the 1930s to enlarge the once scenic lake for water gathering. With its welcoming *Dun Bull Inn* the hamlet at the head of the lake must have been a real haven from the surround of high mountains. Today, dry summers see tourists block the road as they attempt to survey the ever dwindling remains of a silent community.

The old way climbs as a superlative example of an engineered path, such a contrast to many of the ill-devised fell paths of modern times. Splendid ravines on the right feature some impressive waterfalls, notably on Hopgill Beck. The path rises past a pair of ruinous stone huts, the upper one being a perfect foreground to those views back over the lake. From here the going eases and the way becomes a little fainter, but still sufficiently clear and marked by occasional cairns and stakes.

Selside Pike rises across the marsh to our right, with Branstree beyond it. Eschew any ideas of a bee-line, and instead enjoy this delightful path as it winds across the upland amphitheatre to the watershed with Swindale. Drop down just a couple of minutes to find a path branching right: this rises clearly up the fell, though is more a legacy of the farmer's quad bike than earlier fellwalkers. Grand views look into the green floor of secluded Swindale, while to the right are glimpses of Haweswater.

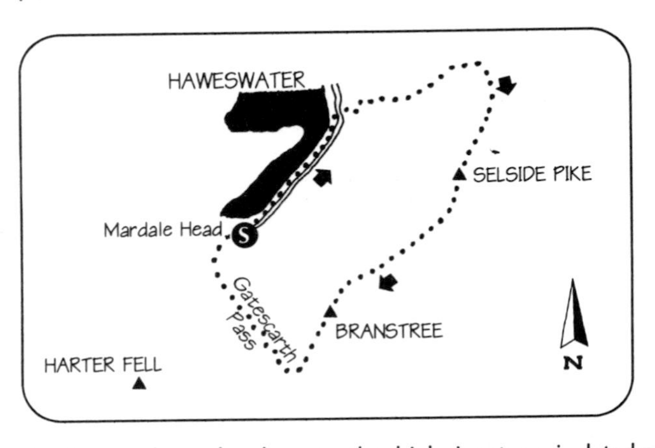

At a fork keep right on the clearer path which rises to an isolated peat fringe defending the summit. The thinning path finds a natural gap, just above which the summit cairn suddenly appears, at a fence corner. From this great pile of stones supporting a large shelter cairn the Lakeland scene is severely restricted by the High Street group, so attention is likely to be diverted to the far horizons of the North Pennines across the Eden Valley, with settlements such as Shap and Penrith discernible.

Head away to the right with the fence for a speedy descent to the saddle of Captain Whelter Bog. It will quickly be realised that this is not a true ridge route, for the fence takes a direct line across the upper flank of an intervening top (2208ft/673m). Those desperate to visit this minor top can easily take it in, but a decent path faithfully shadows the fence to arrive beneath the next, more obvious saddle. Ahead is a prominent beacon on Artle Crag, Branstree, while up to the left is a pillar built by Manchester Corporation to mark the line of its aqueduct.

The path shadows the fence up Branstree's gentle slope, though at the top a detour right to the rash of stones and imposing pillar on Artle Crag is recommended. From here a trod runs directly to the summit, just 40 yards from the fence's junction with a wall. It lives down to expectations by being grassy and exceedingly flat. An insignificant cairn indicates the highest blade of grass, with excitement provided by the discovery of an Ordnance Survey trig. point at ground level.

Rejoin the fence at the wall end, and a thin green trod descends with it. Two initialled boundary stones are passed, one carved atop a small boulder. There are good views into the recesses of Longsleddale, with Morecambe Bay shimmering behind; and Harter Fell is increasingly dominant ahead. Ten minutes has the summit of the Gatescarth Pass underfoot: the track is found just a few yards up the other side of the saddle, which is merely a bog. For an extension onto Harter Fell, see WALK 25. Turn right for a rapid descent, the old road engaging numerous zigzags as it shadows Gatescarth Beck down beneath the frowning crags of Harter Fell, on the left. At the bottom the old road runs down past a small plantation to return to the car park.

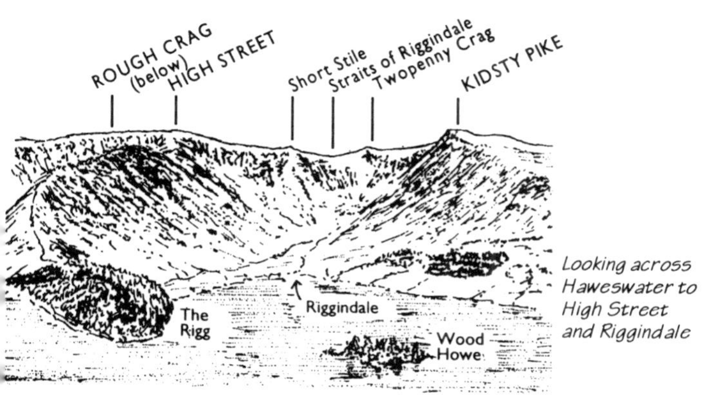

Looking across Haweswater to High Street and Riggindale

25 HARTER FELL

SUMMITS
HARTER FELL 2552ft/778m

START *Mardale Head* ***Grid ref.*** *NY 469107*

DISTANCE *4 miles/6½km* ***ASCENT*** *1758ft/536m*

ORDNANCE SURVEY MAPS
1:50,000 - Landranger 90 *1:25,000 - Outdoor Leisure 5* ***or*** *7*

ACCESS *Start from the road end car park at the head of Haweswater. Buses from Penrith at weekends and Bank Holidays, May to August.*

Harter Fell hovers imposing above the head of Mardale, demanding to be climbed. This straightforward walk makes use of popular passes on either side of the mountain, the return one being a real gem.

S Leave the car park by the kissing-gate at the end, noting an old MCWW (Manchester Corporation Water Works) sign alongside. The broad path runs on to a three-way split at a wall corner. Take the most obvious, left-hand branch, which is our route to the summit of the Gatescarth Pass. This broad, stony way rises past a small plantation and up onto the fell, with Gatescarth Beck for company on the left. The way is infallible as it climbs, often in zigzags, beneath the frowning crags of Harter Fell to the crest of the pass.

The track actually keeps a few yards to the right of the true crest, which is merely a marshy bog. However, our route leaves the track just before the gate, and a broad, stony path climbs to the right. It slants up the flank of Adam Seat (occupied by an initialled boundary stone) onto easier ground, meeting the watershed fence which made the detour over Adam Seat. The fence now remains as company for a foolproof route to the top. Haweswater quickly appears, increasingly expansively, while Kentmere Pike and Harter Fell's summit are seen close by to the left.

Very gentle going leads to a corner of the fence on the north-eastern ridge of the fell, which marks the best viewpoint over Haweswater. Resume with the fence for a few minutes' similarly graded ascent to the wrought-iron embellished summit cairn. Surprisingly, Harter Fell's attractions do not extend to its summit, whose bizarre cairn is insufficient recompense for the grassy plateau denying any intimate views. Features to the south, which will soon be gone from sight, include the slender cone of Ill Bell, and more distantly Morecambe Bay and the peak of Ingleborough in the Yorkshire Dales.

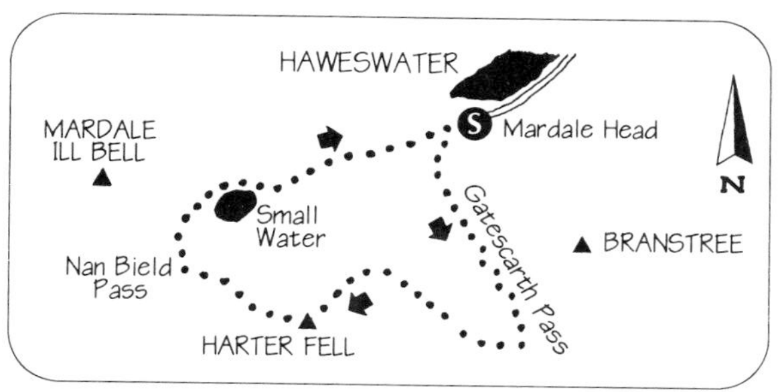

Depart by heading west from the cairn, leaving the security of the fence and initially having no path at all on this bare top. One soon forms however, aided by cairns, and a short stony drop leads down to the narrow defile of the Nan Bield Pass. A sturdy shelter occupies the spot, a unique feature for a Lakeland pass: the names *Mardale* and *Kentmere* are etched into it. This is surely the finest of all Lakeland's passes, and a major walkers' crossroads.

Turn right for a stirring descent to Small Water, which immediately appears below. The old pony track engages artful zigzags through grand surrounds to reach the shore of the tarn. Looking back up from the shore, the upper path is so well made that its presence cannot be detected. On the left of the path stands a trio of stone huts, some form of shelter dating from packhorse times. Small Water is a classic mountain tarn, one of the very finest, and its location beneath the craggy wall of Mardale Ill Bell is best appreciated when seen from the outflow. Crossing the beck, the path quickly leaves this grand scene behind, to be faced by another one as the upper finger of Haweswater appears below. The path keeps company with the lively beck before slanting down to a gate, then on through a moraine field and one last pasture back to the path junction just yards short of the end.

TABLE OF SUMMITS

	FELL	FEET	METRES	
1	HELVELLYN M	3117	950	....
2	Nethermost Pike #	2923	891	....
3	CATSTYCAM	2920	890	....
4	RAISE	2897	883	....
5	FAIRFIELD M	2864	873	....
6	Striding Edge #•	2831	863	....
7	WHITE SIDE	2831	863	....
8	DOLLYWAGGON PIKE	2815	858	....
9	GREAT DODD	2812	857	....
10	STYBARROW DODD	2766	843	....
11	SAINT SUNDAY CRAG M	2759	841	....
12	HIGH STREET M	2717	828	....
13	HART CRAG	2697	822	....
14	HIGH RAISE	2631	802	....
15	GREEN SIDE •	2608	795	....
16	DOVE CRAG	2598	792	....
17	RAMPSGILL HEAD	2598	792	....
18	THORNTHWAITE CRAG	2572	784	....
19	Kidsty Pike #	2559	780	....
20	HARTER FELL	2552	778	....
21	RED SCREES M	2546	776	....
22	CAUDALE MOOR M	2503	763	....
23	The Knott #	2424	739	....
24	CLOUGH HEAD	2382	726	....
25	Birkhouse Moor #	2356	718	....
26	BRANSTREE	2339	713	....
27	Gray Crag #	2293	699	....
28	SHEFFIELD PIKE	2215	675	....
29	PLACE FELL M	2155	657	....
30	SELSIDE PIKE	2149	655	....
31	Middle Dodd #	2145	654	....
32	LITTLE HART CRAG	2090	637	....
33	ROUGH CRAG •	2060	628	....
34	Hartsop Dodd #	2028	618	....
35	St. Raven's Edge •	1945	593	....
36	Hartsop above How	1909	582	....
37	Angletarn Pikes	1860	567	....
38	Brock Crags	1840	561	....
39	Swineside Knott •	1814	553	....
40	Arthur's Pike	1745	532	....
41	Bonscale Pike	1719	524	....
42	High Hartsop Dodd	1701	519	....
43	Birk Fell •	1680	512	....
44	Beda Fell	1670	509	....
45	Gowbarrow Fell	1578	481	....
46	Glenridding Dodd	1450	442	....
47	Arnison Crag	1420	433	....
48	Steel Knotts	1417	432	....
49	Hallin Fell M	1273	388	....

KEY

For walkers who like their hills to be classified:

UPPER CASE - 2000ft fells with at least 100ft/30m of re-ascent ('HEWITT')

- minor 2000ft fells • - non 'WAINWRIGHT' fells

M - fells with at least 500ft/150m of re-ascent ('MARILYN')

LOG OF THE WALKS

WALK	DATE	NOTES
1		
2		
3		
4		
5		
6		
7		
8		
9		
10		
11		
12		
13		
14		
15		
16		
17		
18		
19		
20		
21		
22		
23		
24		
25		

INDEX

Summits and other principle features

Walk number refers; Start points in bold